HANDMADE BASKETS

by Lyn Siler

Watercolors and Illustrations
by Carolyn Kemp

A Sterling/**Lark** Book
Sterling Publishing Co., Inc., New York

CONTENTS

Editor: Carol Taylor
Design: Marcia Winters
Photography: Evan Bracken
Art Direction for Location Photography: Diane Weaver
Production: Elaine Thompson and Marcia Winters

Library of Congress Cataloging-in-Publication Data
Siler, Lyn.
   Handmade baskets ; 28 beautiful baskets to make for your
   home / by Lyn Siler ; watercolors and illustrations by
   Carolyn Kemp.
       p. cm.
   "A Sterling/Lark book."
   Includes bibliographical references and index.
   ISBN 0-8069-8362-0
   1. Basket making.   I. Title
TT879.B3S56   1991
746.41'2--dc20   91-9065
                                    CIP

10 9 8

A Sterling/Lark Book

Produced by Altamont Press, Inc.
50 College Street, Asheville, NC 28801

First paperback edition published in 1992 by
Sterling Publishing Company, Inc.
387 Park Avenue South, New York, N.Y. 10016

© 1991 by Lyn Siler

Distributed in Canada by Sterling Publishing
% Canadian Manda Group, P.O. Box 920, Station U
Toronto, Ontario, Canada M8Z 5P9
Distributed in Great Britain and Europe by Cassell PLC
Villiers House, 41/47 Strand, London WC2N 5JE, England
Distributed in Australia by Capricorn Link Ltd.
P.O. Box 665, Lane Cove, NSW 2066

Every effort has been made to ensure that all the information in
this book is accurate. However, due to differing conditions, tools,
and individual skills, the publisher cannot be responsible for any
injuries, losses, and other damages which may result from the use
of the information in this book.

Printed in Hong Kong by Oceanic Graphic Printing

Sterling   ISBN 0-8069-8362-0   Trade
                0-8069-8363-9   Paper

FOREWORD

Of one thing I am certain. Anyone who weaves, collects or just plain appreciates baskets is a breed apart. Just browse any street fair. If there's a basketmaker's stall, you'll spot us flocking around it like hummingbirds at a feeder, our eyes glazed and our hands reaching out for their latest tactile thrill. One wag compares it to a landlubber's version of "rapture of the deep."

My own addiction began years ago, when Lyn Siler was still playing hopscotch and hadn't even envisioned her first finger callus.

Newly divorced and really strapped, I was faced with a choice. What I needed was an electric coffee percolator. But I also yearned for a handsome straw pot basket I'd been eyeing in a local shop window for several weeks. Needless to say, I went for the pot basket. When I confessed this to my senior editor, a man of great erudition ("Every room should have at least one touch of elegant black" was but one of his maxims), he gave me a pat on the back and said, "It's what any editor worth his salt would have done." Given that shove in the right direction, I've never looked back.

Thirty years and several hundred baskets later, fate (a.k.a. old age) plunked me down, via retirement, in the western North Carolina mountains within proximity of Lyn Siler. Lyn, by then, had become to basketry what M. F. K. Fisher is to the art of eating—and

earned *a lot* of calluses!

In between, however, I continued my basket binge. For several years of living dangerously, I even operated my own retail basket emporium. This was well before baskets became "in," so to speak, before "country" had been emblazoned on a dozen magazine titles (and become a decor stereotype) and when "crafts" surfaced only at church Christmas bazaars.

Basketry in the United States still awaited its resurgence, so it was a matter of scrounging around abroad for baskets—then hoping they wouldn't unravel before hitting the custom house.

I developed a particular fondness for Romanian baskets. They were plain, no-nonsense, peasant baskets reminiscent of our early American ones. Rather than split oak or honeysuckle, Romanians used what *they* had—unpeeled willow, so freshly cut that it wasn't surprising to see baskets sprout pussywillows in high humidity. Amazing.

Another weaver, in Ghana, turned out baskets lush with the joyous and vibrant colors one associates with tribal Africa, the likes of which I haven't seen since.

And then were was "Granny" Reed, octogenarian, lifelong mountaineer and basket weaver. Whenever she needed money for a chaw, she'd get her arthritic hands going, fashion a couple of baskets and tote them into town to sell. Her baskets are hard to describe—sort of a cross between an attache case and a tote, very

primitive, downright homely, in fact. But every time I look at mine I can envision a hundred years of pioneer heritage woven into it. And I love it.

Poor Granny. I'm told that before she died she'd become a little confused. Still having her chaw, she'd sit outside on the stoop of her modest shack, open the front (and only) door and spit her tobacco juice *inside*.

I've also been blessed with a daughter of determination. Although her penchant tends toward spatterware and English Chippendale, she's swooped down on what surely must be every attic and antique shop in New England, ferreting out prized baskets for my next birthday, Father's Day or Christmas.

By now, I like to think a measure of refinement has set in, and I concentrate on the purity of Appalachian basketry and the intricacies of Chinese wedding baskets. A strange pairing, perhaps, but there it is.

At long last, and thus circuitously, when I finally reached Lyn Siler I'd worn out a number of coffeemakers and she was firmly established in the vanguard of Our Great American Craft. And lo and behold, she was going to teach a class! I promptly enrolled.

Like thousands of others, I had read and admired her books. But I wasn't prepared for the lady herself. Now here was one spiffy-lookin' gal! Not only that, she was a born teacher willing to share her expertise as one of the country's prima weavers. The same warmth, humor and ability to communicate that resonate

throughout her books are only heightened in person. I became her cult member on the spot! In retrospect, I was pretty much all thumbs when it came to actually making a basket, but she forced a credible basket or two out of me—and engendered in me a deeper appreciation for those whose work is far more skillful.

Now we welcome her latest volume. In it—for the first time, so far as I know—Lyn adroitly manages to bring a sense of order to the present sprung mattress-like diversity of American basketry. Regional characteristics are sorted out, period styles identified and affable commentaries applied. Accessible instructions are also supplied for making your own basket, should you care to replicate one from any section. It's a treasury!

Once again, the text is beautifully abetted by Carolyn Kemp's illustrations. A basket fancier herself, Carolyn has gained renown as a water colorist par excellence of baskets and other rural artifacts. Here, her depiction of the how-to's lends wonderful clarity to the instructions.

"Feed a fever…" they say. For anyone with the slightest hint of basketmania, this book will do for the spirit what the aroma of fresh brewing coffee can never do. Believe me.

For Americana, give it a capital A.

—James Howe
Old Thickety, North Carolina

Mr. Howe, sometime writer and editor, admits to being a fulltime basket freak.

A generation ago, the handmade baskets of our childhoods were relegated to attics, basements and outbuildings to gather dust and dry rot, by young moderns in search of the "new and surely must be better." They were replaced with colorful, throw-away containers that slowly but surely gorged our waste facilities to overflowing because they didn't "return to dust."

Fortunately, in recent years we have reassessed our values and realized that indestructibility was only one of the infractions of those polyethylene marvels. They were also totally devoid of charm. We have finally realized that all those neat old things in Grandmother's house did more than clutter. Crocheted table scarves, hand-pieced and stitched quilts, handmade, real wood baskets—they were all "little bits of herself" that gave her home the warmth and ambience that ours, with its store-bought things, somehow lacked.

The baskets were especially important. What object evokes more nostalgic memories of the past? Who doesn't remember a favorite Easter basket, or a tall wicker one that sat in the parlor filled with flowers, or a crudely made oak laundry basket?

Finally, they have been pulled out of their hiding places, even garbage dumps, and given places of honor in our homes as valued art objects. They grace many a wall and shelf and hang from exposed beams, lending their surroundings warmth and charm.

In many cases, we have assigned them new and original uses. The basket that in years past carried cotton from the fields now holds toys or magazines. The small basket that would have once carried newly gathered berries may hold toiletries or hand towels.

While traditional baskets have enjoyed a rebirth and will never go out of style, today's basketmakers are perhaps more adventurous than their predecessors. Everyone cannot have, or doesn't want, old baskets. For those of us who want to fill our homes with little bits of ourselves, basketmaking is a natural. What is more gratifying than making, with your own hands, something that can be useful as well as decorative? Whether you feel your baskets are art pieces or functional accents, the end result will be highly prized.

This book is intended to be a catalyst, to trigger in your imagination all the possibilities of baskets you can make for your home, whatever your decor. There are frilly baskets that call for a Victorian setting. Some are authentic Southwest Indian baskets and others use colors typical of that region, allowing them to blend into a Southwestern decor. There are instructions for making traditional Early American baskets to fit into a Primitive or American Country home. In the Country European section are baskets typical of a European setting, either in their motif or in their entirety. And for those of us who just like a creative mixture, there is the Eclectic section. An eclectic decorating scheme could, of course, absorb any of the baskets in the book.

Use this book as a guide. Employ the techniques and methods, but by all means vary them to fit your needs. You will be amazed by your own creative ability. Whatever the style of your home, there is something here for you. There are no hard and fast rules for where a particular basket must be used; they are categorized here partly for the sake of organization. The love of baskets is universal, as is their use. Use the ones you like anywhere you want, and enjoy both making them and using them for years to come.

G L O S S A R Y

aging The process that occurs when a basket turns dark from natural environmental elements.

arrow Two rows of weaving that form an arrow pattern. Consists of one row of regular weave, a step-up, a reverse weave and ending.

ash splints Strips of ash that are thinned enough to use for stakes or weavers.

awl A tool resembling an ice pick used for opening spaces and making holes in reed. It is shorter than an ice pick and not as sharply pointed.

base The bottom of a basket; woven mat.

bevel To cut a square edge to a sloping edge; scarf.

bow-knot ear A four-point lashing ear, wrapped only once and "tied" in front.

binder cane Cane that is wider than regular strand cane; used recently to lash basket rims in place.

bi-spokes Extra or added spokes, inserted beside the original ones.

braided God's Eye A four-point lashing like the regular God's Eye except it is interwoven and appears braided to the eye; woven God's Eye.

braided handle Any of several different methods of interweaving the reed around the handle; specifically, the wheat braid.

brake A short piece of reed woven alternately above the beginning of a weaver to hold it in place.

butt To bring the ends of any two pieces together, flush against each other.

cane The outer peel of rattan, used in weaving as an embellishment and on chair bottoms.

chain pairing The same as pairing or twined arrows.

chase weave A method of weaving with two weavers at once. Continuous weaving over an even number of stakes. The weaver moves first, and the chaser (the other weaver) follows alternately.

coil One row of waling that ends with a step-up and a lock.

coiling A weaving technique using an inner core which is wrapped solidly with a smaller thread.

continuous weave Weaving done over an odd number of stakes. It is not done one row at a time, but rather continuously from beginning to end, with weavers added periodically.

D handle A basket handle that continues across the bottom of the basket and that, turned on its side, resembles the letter D.

diagonal weave A method of weaving in which the elements interweave with themselves. Also called diagonal plaiting and oblique weaving.

double-bottom A method of construction in which one base is woven and a second (woven) one is placed on top of the first.

dyeing Coloring reed with any number of natural or commercial dyes.

ear (1) weaving or lashing done at the intersecting point of the rim and handle that holds the two pieces securely. (2) lashing into which the ribs are inserted. (3) loops that join a swing handle to the basket.

embellishment Any decorative treatment done to the handle or body of a basket that is not essential to its construction.

fanny The twin, gizzard-shaped bottom of an egg basket; buttocks.

filling in On some ribbed baskets a wedge-shaped area remains unwoven when the rim is full; it must be filled in by some type of "back and forth" weaving; also called "packing."

five-point lashing A lashing (ear) done around any five intersecting pieces.

frame The support (usually wood) around which the basket is woven.

French randing A strong diagonal randing pattern that uses short rods (weavers) that are begun at the base one at a time.

God's Eye A four-point lashing; ear.

grapevine A vine used for weaving baskets and handles.

hairs The splinters from the reed that usually occur from overuse, to be clipped or singed when the basket is finished.

handle The part of the basket by which it is carried.

honeysuckle A wild vine used for weaving baskets, smaller than grapevine.

hoop Ring or piece of wood shaped into a circle; machine or handmade, present

Indian weave   in ribbed baskets.
A method of continuous weaving over an even number of stakes/spokes, adjusted each round by weaving over two spokes so the alternate over/under pattern resumes.

Japanese weave   Weaving over two spokes and under one.

lasher   The piece of reed that wraps around and secures all the rim pieces together.

lashing   The act of wrapping all the rim pieces or wrapping the ear; the pieces of reed used to wrap are also referred to as lashing.

loop   An ear that holds the swing handle and pushes down into the basket.

losing a lasher   A means of hiding the end of the reed in the rim or in the weaving.

mat   The woven base of a flat basket.

notch   The indented space on a push-in handle made to fit under the rim and prevent the handle from pulling out.

oak splints   Strips of oak wood thinned enough to use as stakes or weavers; also called splits.

oblique weave   Diagonal plaiting or weaving.

osier   Any of various willows that have tough, flexible twigs or branches which are used for wicker work.

packing   (1) pushing each row snugly down beside the previously woven row. (2) a method of building up or filling in an area by turning one spoke sooner each row.

pairing   Twining.

plain weave   Over-one, under-one weave; randing.

plaited   Woven.

pre-form   Shaped or formed before being used.

randing   A simple over-under weaving with a single weaver and an odd number of stakes.

rattan   A climbing palm (vine) from which reed is made.

reed   The inner core of rattan that has been cut into either flat, round, flat oval, half round, or oval shapes; used for baskets and furniture.

rib   The round or oval pieces that extend from one side of the basket to the other and form the basic skeleton.

rim   The pieces, inside and outside, that fit over the top row of weaving to form an edge and give stability to the sides.

rim filler   A piece of round reed, seagrass or other suitable material that goes between and on top of the two rim pieces.

scarf   A joint in which the ends of any two pieces are cut so they overlap each other and join firmly.

scarfing   To join by cutting the two end pieces, usually beveled or on a slant, so they fit together smoothly.

seagrass   A twisted rope of grass suitable for weaving.

shaper   An instrument used for shaving away wood; a small rasp.

sight   To look at a basket frame and determine the rib lengths to give the desired shape; to eyeball.

slewing   A wicker work weave done with two or more paired weavers in a randing pattern.

slype   A long, mitered (pointed) cut.

spiral   (1) the result of twill weaving (under two, over two) continuously over an odd number of spokes. (2) a gradually widening curve winding away from a base to create a design.

spline   A wedge-shaped reed made primarily for use with pressed cane; also used to make loops and handles in baskets.

splice   The place where two pieces of wood, having been scarfed, overlap.

spoke   The elements, usually round reed, which form the rigid framework of a basket.

staining   A term that has come to mean coloring reed to give it an aged look.

stake   Pieces of the woven mat (base) which are upsett and become the upright elements.

stepping up   A term used in twill weaving meaning to start the next row one stake to the right (or left, as the case may be) of the starting point on the previous row.

stroke   A movement of the weaver.

swing handle   A handle attached to a basket by means of a loop or protruding ear that allows it to swing freely from side to side.

three-point lashing   The wrapping used to cover the intersecting point of any three elements.

Continued on page 142.

T O O L S

Some tools are essential for basketmaking; others are elective. The tape measure, awl, clothespins and pencil are absolute necessities and are easily found around the home. The newer tools on the scene—spoke weight and flex-grip scissors— become essential only after you have used them.

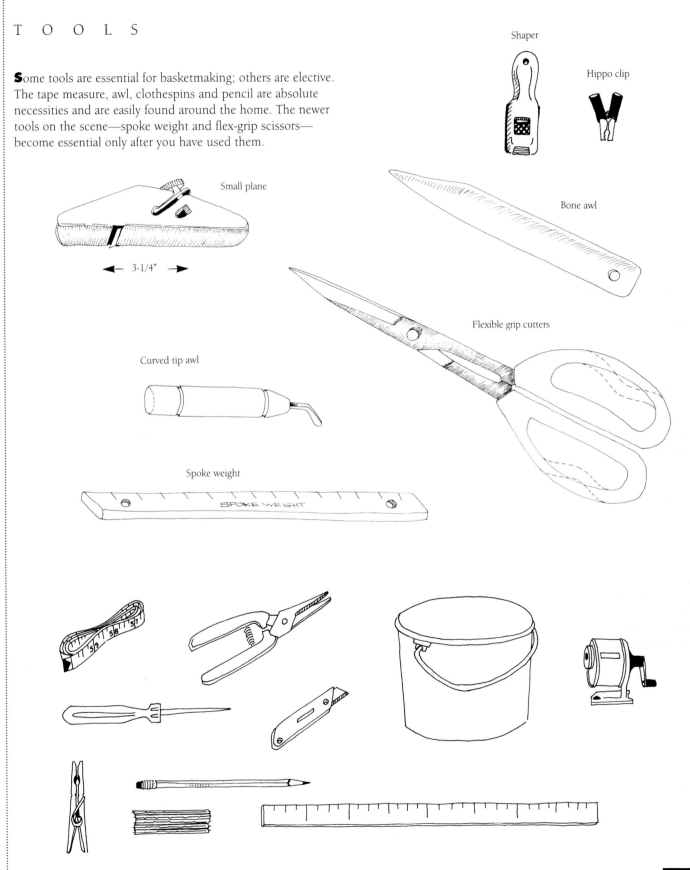

Shaper

Hippo clip

Small plane

← 3-1/4" →

Bone awl

Flexible grip cutters

Curved tip awl

Spoke weight

SPOKE WEIGHT

Basketry materials have changed very little over the years.
The most frequently used types and sizes are shown here.
All the materials are readily available in craft and hobby
stores and can be purchased by mail order from suppliers
who advertise in craft and home-decorating magazines.

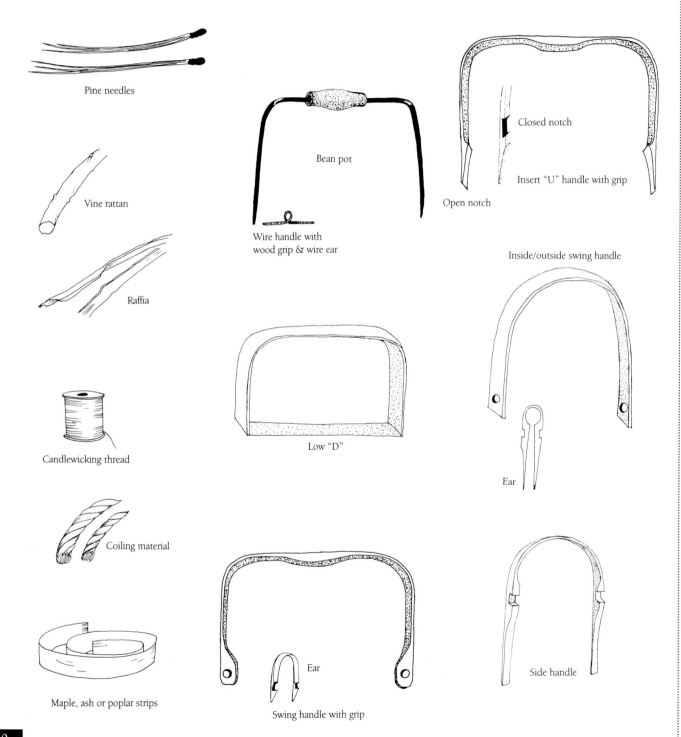

Pine needles

Vine rattan

Raffia

Candlewicking thread

Coiling material

Maple, ash or poplar strips

Bean pot

Wire handle with
wood grip & wire ear

Low "D"

Swing handle with grip

Ear

Closed notch

Open notch

Insert "U" handle with grip

Inside/outside swing handle

Ear

Side handle

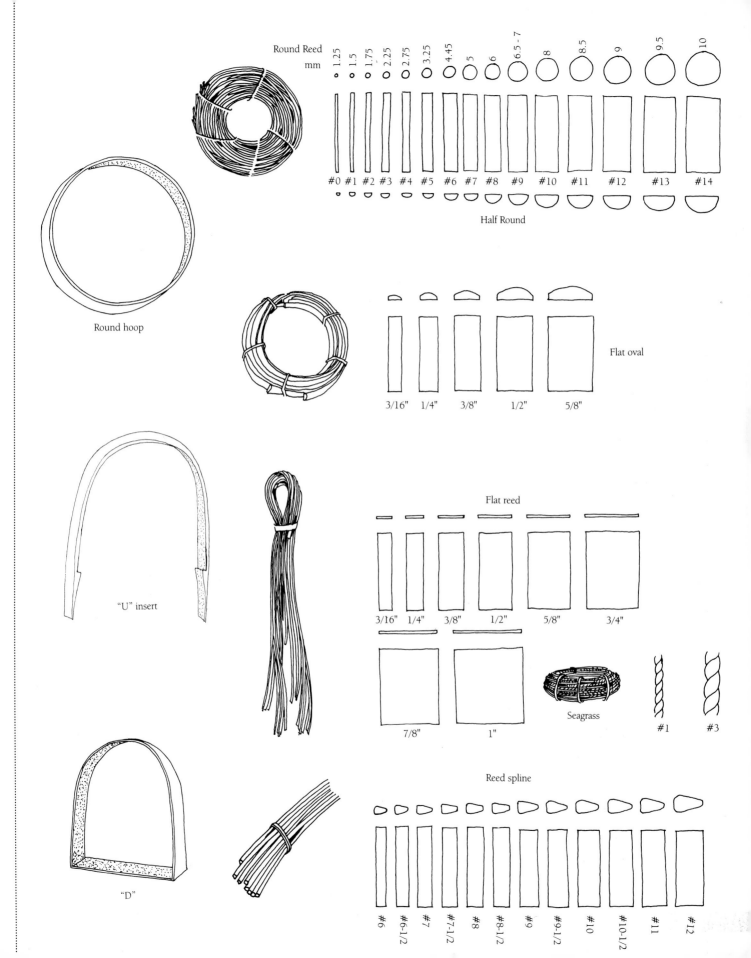

Round Reed
mm

1.25 1.5 1.75 2.25 2.75 3.25 4.45 5 6 6.5 - 7 8 8.5 9 9.5 01

#0 #1 #2 #3 #4 #5 #6 #7 #8 #9 #10 #11 #12 #13 #14

Half Round

Round hoop

Flat oval

3/16" 1/4" 3/8" 1/2" 5/8"

"U" insert

Flat reed

3/16" 1/4" 3/8" 1/2" 5/8" 3/4"

Seagrass

#1 #3

7/8" 1"

Reed spline

"D"

#6 #6-1/2 #7 #7-1/2 #8 #8-1/2 #9 #9-1/2 #10 #10-1/2 #11 #12

Weaving Variations

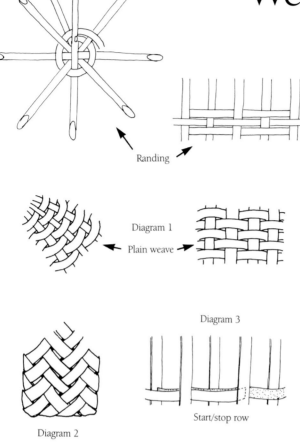

Randing

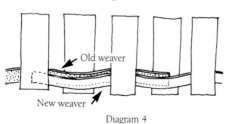

Diagram 1

Plain weave

Diagram 3

Diagram 2

Start/stop row

Adding flat weaver

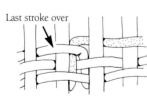

Old weaver

New weaver

Diagram 4

Regardless of the materials being used, weaving is the interlacing of one set of elements with another—the weft with the warp. The warp is the stationary set of elements. When you're working with flat splints, the warp consists of stakes and the weft is made up of weavers. With round reed, the warp consists of the spokes, with the weft again being the weavers. In basketry, weaving takes a number of common forms, including the following.

PLAIN WEAVE

Plain weave is the simplest and most common of all weaves. Each weft element moves over and under the warp element in opposite order, each round. Using round reed, the term for plain weave is randing. See **Diagram 1**.

PLAITING

Plaiting is the general term used in basketry for the interlacing of two flat elements of equal width. Diagonal plaiting is plain weaving with two like elements interwoven at right angles. See **Diagram 2**.

START-STOP WEAVING

Weaving around a base one row at a time, starting and stopping each row, is known as start-stop weaving. Using flat reed, begin the weaver on the outside of the basket on the outside of a stake. Weave around the basket, end by weaving over the starting point and cut the weaver behind the fourth stake. See **Diagram 3**.

CONTINUOUS WEAVES

To weave continuously means to work with one weaver round after round, weaving over the starting point indefinitely. How you add a new weaver depends on the material you're using. If you're working with flat

Last stroke over

Last stroke under

Adding new weaver
with round reed

Diagram 5

Continuous weave over odd # spokes

Diagram 6

Chase weave

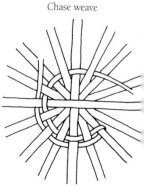

Diagram 7

reed, a new weaver must be added as in **Diagram 4**, slipping the new one under the fourth stake from the end of the old weaver. Weave with both old and new until the old one runs out, then continue with the new one. If you're working with round reed, whether weaving a start-stop row or weaving continuously, a new weaver is added as in **Diagram 5**. The weaver can be ended after an over or under stroke. Some instructions also call for the new weaver to simply be laid beside the old one.

There are several methods of continuous weaving:

1. As in **Diagram 6**, one element will weave around an odd number of stakes (or spokes) in an alternate over/under pattern.

2. In order to successfully work an over/under weave around an even number of stakes (spokes), you must either chase-weave, as in **Diagram 7**, working with first one weaver then the other; or Indian weave, as in **Diagram 8**, by weaving one round, tracing the original path for two or four stakes, and then weaving over two stakes, which puts the weaver in the alternate over/under pattern.

TWILL WEAVES

With flat reed, to "twill" means that a weft element is taken over two or more warp elements and under one or more. It can be accomplished by working continuous or individual start-stop rows. **Diagram 9** shows how to add a new weaver in a continuous twill weave. **Diagram 10** shows the beginning and end of a two/two twill start-stop row. When you're working a continuous twill weave, the total number of stakes (or spokes) is critical. For example, working an over two, under one twill continuously requires a total number of stakes (spokes) that is divisible by three plus or minus one. If the number is minus one, the design will spiral to the right; if it is plus one, the design will spiral to the left. An over three, under two twill must have a total number of stakes that is divisible by five plus one or plus four. It is possible to work a continuous chase twill weave. Working in an over three, under two pattern, the total number of stakes must be divisible by five plus three. For example, 12 stakes by 12 stakes is a total of 48 stakes, which is 45 (which is divisible by five) plus three. An over two, under one pattern may be worked over a total number of stakes that is divisible by three plus one. Continuous twill weaves may be worked over odd numbers as well, in the same formulas that were used for continuous chase weaves.

COILING

Coiling is an extremely tight and rigid method of basket construction executed by using a rigid core that is wrapped and stitched with a softer, more flexible material. Rows of the wrapped core are stacked (coiled) rather than woven. See **Diagram 11**.

TWINING

Note: For simplicity, the terms spoke and stakes are both used, but note that twining, as well as waling, can be done when using either spokes or stakes.

In basketry, twining is usually done with round reed, worked over or around either flat or round reed. See **Diagram 12**. Twining is often used as a locking row around flat bases to hold the stakes in place. To do this,

Coiling

Diagram 11

Twining

Diagram 12

Indian weave

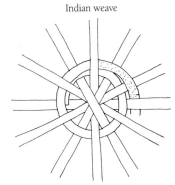

Diagram 8

Twill weave

Diagram 9   Adding new weaver

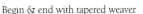

Begin & end with tapered weaver

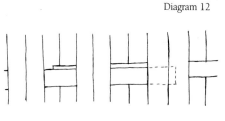

Diagram 10

Twining with 1 weaver

Diagram 13

Twining with 2 weavers

Diagram 14

Twining around corner

Diagram 15

Twining around "D" handle

Diagram 16

Ending twining after 1 row

Diagram 17

Ending twining after multiple rows

Diagram 18

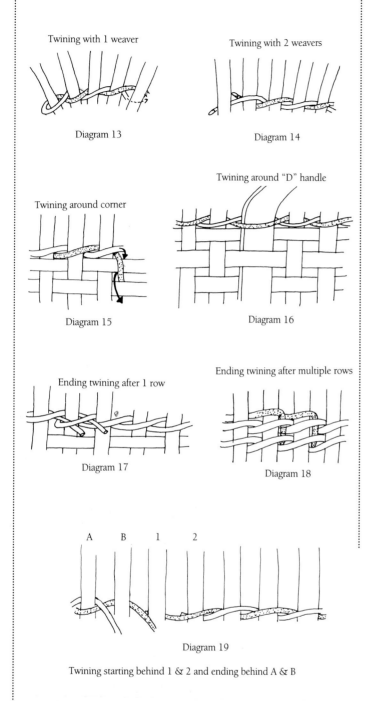

A   B   1   2

Diagram 19

Twining starting behind 1 & 2 and ending behind A & B

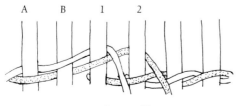

A   B   1   2

Diagram 20

Step-up

begin by either (a) folding a round reed off center, so both weavers don't end at the same time (see **Diagram 13**) or (b) starting two pieces behind consecutive stakes as in **Diagram 14**. Twine around the corners of bases as in **Diagram 15**. Always weave around the corner with the bottom weaver first, then take the top one under. In twining around an upright handle, pretend it is lying flat and weave as you normally would. See **Diagram 16**. To lock a row of twining, push the ends under the row that is already in place as in **Diagram 17**. To end twining after several rows, push the ends into the weaving beside two consecutive spokes or stakes. See **Diagram 18**.

DECORATIVE TWINING ARROW

Step 1: Work one row of plain twining, ending as in **Diagram 19**.

Step 2: Work a "step-up" as in **Diagram 20**. Move the farthest right weaver over

one stake to the right, behind the next and out to the front. Move the other weaver over one stake to the right, behind the next one and out to the front.

Step 3: Work one row of reverse twining. In **Diagram 21**, the left weaver moves next over stake #2, under the right weaver, behind stake #3 and out to the front. Next, the left weaver moves over spoke #3, under the right weaver, behind stake #4 and out to the front. Repeat with each "left weaver."

Step 4: End the row of reverse twining as in **Diagram 22**, taking the ends of both the weavers behind the beginning spokes and going under the weaving already in place. **Diagram 23** shows a single row of reverse twining.

To add a weaver when twining around flat or round reed, push the old end into the twined area beside a spoke after an "over" stroke. Push the end of the new

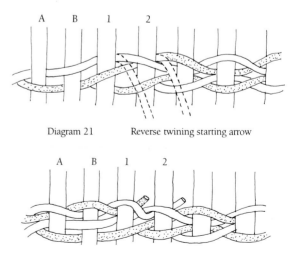

A   B   1   2

Diagram 21   Reverse twining starting arrow

A   B   1   2

Diagram 22   Reverse twining ending arrow

weaver into the weaving beside the spoke before and continue with it. See **Diagram 24**.

WALES

By definition, a wale is a weaving technique in which the leftmost weaver is moved to the right over two or more spokes, behind one and out to the front again.

THREE-ROD WALE

Also known as triple weave, three-rod wale is worked with three weaving elements and started behind three consecutive spokes. Each time, the farthest left weaver is taken over the two spokes to the right, behind the next and out to the front. In **Diagram 25**, the arrow shows the future path of weaver A, which is the farthest left. Next, weaver B will move over two spokes to the right, behind the third stake, and out to the front. Just be sure each time to use the farthest left weaver.

A single row of three-rod wale that ends with a step-up and a lock is called a three-rod coil. It is started as in **Diagram 25**, woven around to the three spokes prior to the starting spokes, as in **Diagram 26**, and then steps up and locks as in **Diagram 27**. To step-up, move the right-most weaver in front of two spokes, behind one and out to the front. Repeat with each of the three weavers. To lock them in place, push the ends, starting with the right weaver first, under the weavers already in place, coming out to the front of the basket. The weaver will end under their own starting places.

FOUR-ROD WALE

Four-Rod wale is worked exactly like three-rod wale, except with four weavers instead of three. Of course, a five-rod wale would simply be worked with five weavers. With any of the wales, the important thing to know is

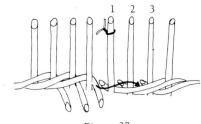

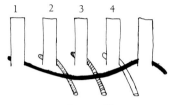

Diagram 27

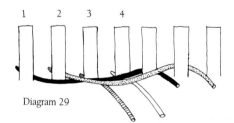

Diagram 28

Diagram 29

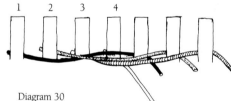

Diagram 30

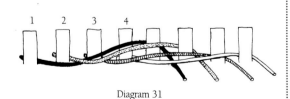

Diagram 31

Reverse twining single row

Diagram 23

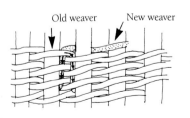
Old weaver   New weaver

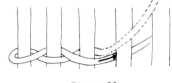

Diagram 24

Adding weaver to twining

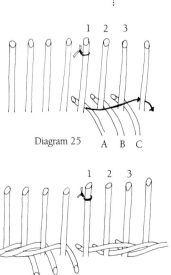

Diagram 25   A   B   C

Diagram 26

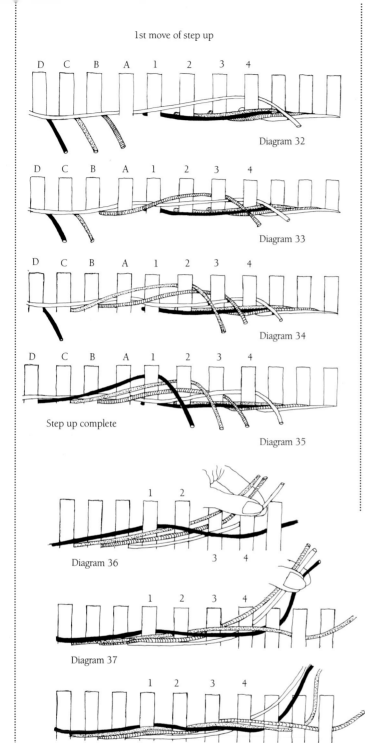

1st move of step up

D C B A 1 2 3 4

Diagram 32

D C B A 1 2 3 4

Diagram 33

D C B A 1 2 3 4

Diagram 34

D C B A 1 2 3 4

Step up complete

Diagram 35

1 2 3 4

Diagram 36

1 2 3 4

Diagram 37

1 2 3 4

Diagram 38

1 2 3 4

Diagram 39

that each weaver is started behind four consecutive spoke (or stakes), and each weaver is taken, in its turn, to the right, over three (in the case of four-rod) spokes, behind the next and out to the front again. See **Diagrams 28** to **31** for an up-close view of each of the four weavers moving in its turn.

FOUR-ROD STEP-UP

A "step-up" is needed if you are going to work a coil and do not want the pattern to spiral. It is a way of repositioning the weavers without continuing the waling. Instead of moving the leftmost weaver, the weaver farthest right moves each stroke in its turn. In **Diagram 32**, the farthest right weaver has moved over three stakes, behind the fourth and is out to the front. In **Diagram 33**, the next weaver, which is now the far-

thest right weaver, has been moved. In **Diagram 34**, the third has moved and in **Diagram 35** all four weavers are in place and the step-up is complete. If you are interested in working a "Four-Rod Arrow," the weavers are now in the correct position to begin.

FOUR-ROD ARROW

A four-rod arrow consists of one row of four-rod wale, a step-up, one row of reverse four-rod wale and a step-up and lock.

To work a four-rod reverse row, move the leftmost weaver, each in its turn, over three stakes, but it must also move under the ends of the other three spokes. Then it continues over the next three stakes, behind the fourth and out to the front. **Diagrams 36** to **39** show each weaver completing the stroke, each one in its turn.

Up Close & Technical

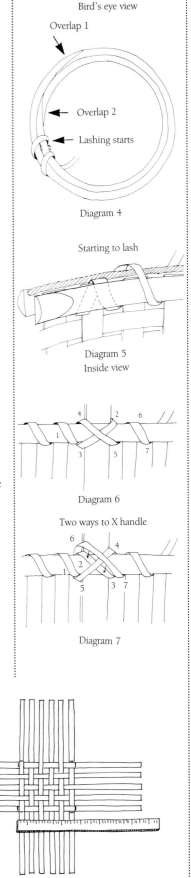

Bird's eye view

Overlap 1

Overlap 2

Lashing starts

Diagram 4

Starting to lash

Diagram 5
Inside view

Diagram 6

Two ways to X handle

Diagram 7

After a decade of teaching basketmaking, I have discovered that a handful of technical problems consistently baffle novices and even more experienced basket weavers. I hope that some of these problem areas can be clarified here.

RIGHT & WRONG SIDE OF REED

The first thing you must know about reed is that, because of the way it is cut, it has a "right" and a "wrong" side. The right side is always smoother and has slightly beveled edges. The wrong side splinters and is "hairy" when bent over the finger. Sometimes the difference is easier to see if the reed is wet. If you encounter reed that is so good you can't decide which side is better, its quality is such that you need not worry which side is up. See **Diagram 1**.

HOW LONG TO SOAK REED

As a general rule, three to five minutes is ample time for soaking reed in warm water. Larger sizes of round reed require longer soaking. For instance, #12 or #15 round reed, used usually for making handles, may require an hour or longer for the entire thickness of the reed to be penetrated.

HOW TO RIM A BASKET

There are quite a few different rimming methods, but one of the most popular to use on splint baskets is the two-piece (flat oval) rim that is lashed in place. A word of explanation about that sort of rim: The ends of the rim pieces, usually flat oval or half-round reed, must be shaved so the overlapped area is no thicker than a single thickness of the reed. Using a knife or a trimming plane, shave about half the thickness from the top of one and the bottom of the other. One piece is placed on the inside of the basket and the other on the outside. See **Diagram 2**. **Diagram 3**

shows the two pieces fitting together with a piece of round reed (filler) between the two rim pieces.

Place the two overlapped areas near, but not on top of, each other. See **Diagram 4**. Begin lashing the rim pieces together just past the two overlapped areas, so that if there is any extra fullness in the rim pieces, it will be worked out at the ends. Begin the lasher as in **Diagram 5**, starting the lasher from the inside of the basket and moving it up under the rim, between the rim and the basket wall. Hook the end over the wall, leaving a tail between the wall and the outside rim. Take the long end of the weaver around the rim, to the next space between the stakes, through and around again.

Should you want to make an X as you cross over the handle, you can do so as shown in **Diagram 6**, by entering the space from the outside of the basket at 1,

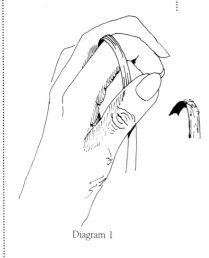

Diagram 1

Diagram 2

One end of rim has been planed down on rounded side of flat oval

Other end of rim has been planed to "leave" rounded side and remove flat side

Diagram 3

Diagram 8

taking the weaver diagonally up behind to 2, down diagonally to 3, up to 4 (inside the basket) and down diagonally to 5. **Diagram 7** shows an alternative method. Follow the numbers in the diagram and trace the weaving path from 6 to 7.

HOW TO TRUE A BASE

Once you've woven the base of a basket, measure it and make any adjustments that are needed. Mark the corners on all sides. See **Diagram 8**.

STEPPING OVER A TWILL WEAVE

This technique is also known as a step-up. The "overs" in each row must move one, two or three (or whatever number) to the right or left of the previous row's "overs." It is particularly difficult for beginners to see where to begin a row. As in **Diagram 9**, a row is woven in an over three, under three pattern. The next row is also starting in an over three, under three pattern, but is stepping over to the right one stake.

DYEING AND STAINING REED

More and more basketmakers are using color in their baskets. There is, to my knowledge, no dye that is really colorfast. To be sure, the safest treatment of dyed baskets is to make sure they are not exposed to direct sunlight or even direct fluorescent lighting for extended periods of time. One possibility of keeping the color brighter for longer is to spray it with a satin or matte clear acrylic sealer.

To dye reed with commercial dyes, follow the manufacturer's directions, usually mixing the contents of the package with one gallon of water. If you want a much lighter tint, add more water or use less of the dye. Test dye pieces until you are satisfied with the color. To make a darker shade, simply use more dye or less water than is specified. For the color to set permanently, the water must be just before boiling. Rinse the reed several times. Some basketmakers find that adding a cup of white vinegar to the final rinse and letting it soak for 30 minutes or longer helps to set the dye.

Should you want an aged look for your baskets, consider using a brown or gray dye and dipping the entire basket, or making your own stain from walnut hulls. It is totally natural and, unlike oil-based stains, leaves no offensive odor. If you have access to walnuts, either use the entire nut with the hull (just as it falls from the tree) or remove the nut and use only the outer hull. The shell is useless, but the outer green hull contains so much dye that if you aren't careful you will have stained fingers very quickly. Confine the hulls in some synthetic fabric (nylon and polyester are good) so they don't disintegrate and cover them with water. In a few days, you will have a nice brown stain. If you are in a hurry and want a stain immediately, place the hulls in a pan, cover them with water and heat to boiling. Simmer the hulls until the water is brown. Pour the stain over the basket or submerge the basket in the stain.

Pecan (and the hulls from other nuts) will also produce a stain, but more hulls are required, as they have less oil.

Dyeing variegated reed has become quite popular. To "space dye" reed, coil individually all the strips of reed to be dyed, and tie each coil loosely. Mix and heat four colors of dye. Looking at **Diagram 10**, dip the coil into the first dye at 6:00, the second dye at 12:00, the third at 3:00 and the fourth at 9:00, allowing the colors to overlap each other for about 1". Almost any combination of colors is nice. Don't be afraid to experiment.

HOW TO DETERMINE LENGTHS FOR YOUR OWN CREATIONS

Simple! First determine the overall size you want the basket to be. For example, let's make a basket 10" wide by 16" long by 6" deep. To obtain the length measurement, add the base length (16") and the depth of each side (6" on each side = 12"), plus 3" on each side for tucking at the top. Therefore: 16" + 12" + 6" = 34".

To get the width measurement, add the base width (10") and the depth of each side (6" each side = 12"), plus the same 6" for tucking: 10" + 12" + 6" = 28".

To determine what size reed to use, draw off the area and use a ruler to learn how many pieces of each to use. Don't forget to allow for approximately 3/8" between stakes. The amount of space between stakes is determined by the size reed with which you will weave. The narrower the weaving material, the smaller the space. Likewise, the larger the weaving material, the wider the space between stakes. As a general rule, the space between stakes should be only slightly larger than the weavers. See **Diagram 11**.

Diagram 9

Diagram 10

12:00

9:00   3:00

6:00

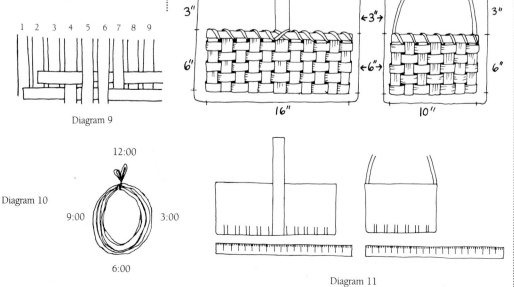

Diagram 11

EARLY AMERICAN

Market Basket

Historically, any basket that has a flat bottom and is square or rectangular has been broadly classified as a market basket. The possibilities are endless for changing designs and colors of the market basket. The instructions presented here will produce the plainly woven (no color) rectangular basket. At the end of these instructions, you will find general measurements for making the others pictured. Consider some of these designs, then create your own to match your decor.

APPROXIMATE SIZE
8" x 12" x 12" high

MATERIALS
5/8" flat reed (stakes)
3/8" flat reed (fillers & weavers)
#2 round reed (twining)
1/2" flat oval reed (rim)
Seagrass (filler)
3/16" flat oval (lashing)
8" x 12" D handle

WEAVING THE BASE
From the 5/8" flat reed, cut 7 stakes 32" long and 10 stakes 28" long. From the 3/8" flat reed, cut 6 filler pieces 18" long.

Soak all the pieces until they are pliable. Mark the centers of all the pieces on the rough side.

Lay 4 of the 32" pieces vertically on a flat surface, aligning the center marks. Place the D handle across (perpendicular to) the 4 pieces, covering the center marks. Align the center of the handle with the center space (between the second and third stakes). See **Diagram 1**.

Next, lay 3 more 32" pieces vertically on top of the handle. Also, lay the 3/8" (22" long) pieces on each side of the 5/8" pieces. See **Diagram 2**.

Next, weave the 24" pieces vertically through the ones you have placed horizontally. *Note:* Treat the filler pieces as one with the 5/8" pieces they lie between. Place a spoke weight or heavy book across one end of the stakes while weaving the other end.

Looking at **Diagram 3**, weave the first 28" stake to the right of the handle, going under the first vertical piece, over the next 3, under the next, etc. Continue to weave in the 28" pieces, alternating "overs" and "unders" every row as in **Diagram 3**. Weave 5 pieces to the right of the handle and 5 pieces to the left. The first piece to the left of the handle should be woven identically to the one on the right. When all the base pieces are woven in, measure

and true the base to 8" x 12".

Bend all the filler (22") pieces over to the inside of the base and tuck them under the third vertical "over" piece. Cut any pieces that are too long so they will hide under the stake. See **Diagram 4**.

MAKING A LOCKING ROW
Soak a long piece of #2 round reed until it is pliable. Fold it a little off center and begin twining as in **Diagram 5**. Loop the fold around one of the stakes coming from under the woven base, taking the top weaver under the next stake each time. Try to imagine the handle as another stake and twine around it too. *Note:* If you have a problem with twining consult the "Up Close" section for assistance.

Twine around the base,

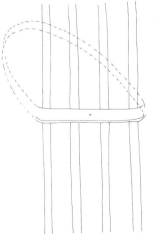

Diagram 1

Diagram 2

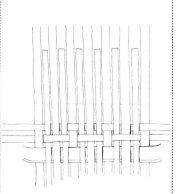

Diagram 3

pushing the twining as close as possible against the base. Tuck the ends under the beginning and cut. *Note:* If you wish, the twining row may be removed once the sides are woven or you may leave it in place.

WEAVING THE SIDES

Rewet the stakes if they have dried. Upsett the sides by bending each stake over on itself toward the center of the basket. They will not stand, but the crease at the base of the stake is important. See **Diagram 6**.

Soak a long piece of 3/8" flat reed. Begin weaving start-stop rows as follows:

Making the stakes stand upright, place the end of the weaver, right side out, against the outside of a stake. See **Diagram 7**. Weave over 1, under 1 around the basket. Upon returning to the starting point, weave over the beginning of the weaver to the fourth stake. Cut the weaver in the middle of the fourth stake. It will be hidden when the next row is woven and the fourth stake

stands up-right. Weave 14 start-stop rows, beginning and ending each one as the first. Also, begin and end each row in a different place. Turn the basket 1/4 turn before you begin each row. This will avoid a build-up of thickness from the overlapped areas.

FINISHING THE BASKET

As in **Diagram 8**, notice which stakes are on the inside of the top row of weaving. Cut those stakes flush with the top row of

weaving. Point the ones on the outside, rewet them, if necessary, bend them over to the inside and tuck them behind the first available row of weaving.

Soak 2 pieces of 1/2" flat oval reed, both long enough to reach around the basket and overlap by 3". Also soak a long piece of 3/16" flat oval

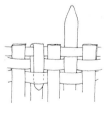

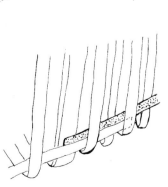

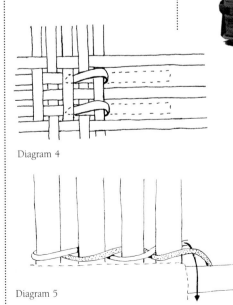

Diagram 4

Diagram 5

Diagram 6

Diagram 7

Diagram 8

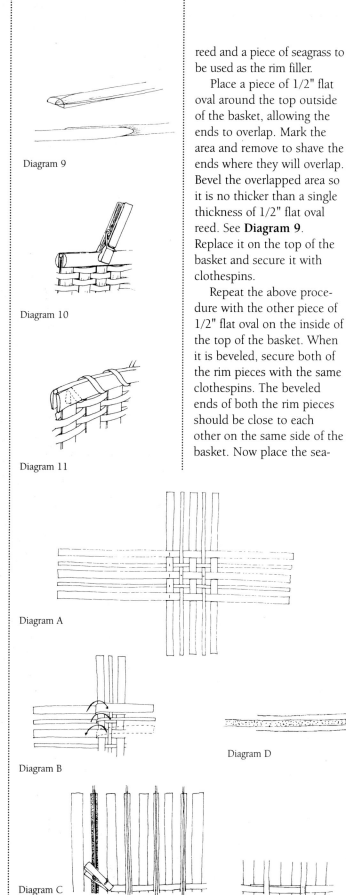

Diagram 9

Diagram 10

Diagram 11

Diagram A

Diagram B

Diagram C

reed and a piece of seagrass to be used as the rim filler.

Place a piece of 1/2" flat oval around the top outside of the basket, allowing the ends to overlap. Mark the area and remove to shave the ends where they will overlap. Bevel the overlapped area so it is no thicker than a single thickness of 1/2" flat oval reed. See **Diagram 9**. Replace it on the top of the basket and secure it with clothespins.

Repeat the above procedure with the other piece of 1/2" flat oval on the inside of the top of the basket. When it is beveled, secure both of the rim pieces with the same clothespins. The beveled ends of both the rim pieces should be close to each other on the same side of the basket. Now place the sea-grass between the 2 rim pieces. See **Diagram 10**. You are now ready to lash the rim to the basket.

Begin lashing just past the area where the rim pieces overlap. Push the end of the lasher up between the rim pieces and hook it over the basket wall to secure it. Lash all the rim components to the basket, as in **Diagram 11**, going through the spaces between all the stakes. End the lashing by hiding the ends between the rim pieces or inside the basket behind a weaver.

TO MAKE THE PLAID MARKET BASKET

(Shown on opposite page)
- Dye 1/2" flat reed burgundy
- Dye 7/8" flat reed hunter green
- Dye 1/4" flat reed hunter green

From the 1/2" burgundy reed, cut 2 pieces 37" long and 6 pieces 30" long. From the 7/8" green reed, cut 3 pieces 37" long and 5 pieces 30" long. From the natural 11/64" flat reed, cut 8 pieces 10" long.

Lay the 37" long pieces horizontally, alternating sizes. Weave the 30" long

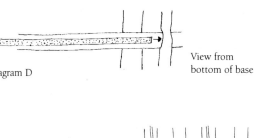

Diagram D

View from bottom of base

Diagram E

pieces vertically. See **Diagram A**. Upsett the sides as in **B**. Weave the sides in the following:
- 4 rows of 3/8" natural reed
- 4 rows of 1/4" green reed
- 2 rows of 1/2" burgundy reed
- 1 row of 7/8" green reed
- 2 rows of 1/2" burgundy reed
- 4 rows of 1/4" green reed
- 5 rows of 3/8" natural

All rows are woven in start-stop method. See **Diagram C** for how to start and stop rows overlapping the ends for 4 stakes. After the first 4 rows of natural 3/8" flat are woven, insert the 11/64" pieces on top of the burgundy stakes as in **Diagrams C & D**, going behind the 3/8" natural and under 1 stake on the bottom of the basket. Weave one 11/64" piece around the basket with the 7/8" green weaver as in **Diagram E**.

Follow the general instructions for the market basket for finishing stakes and applying rim. Before the rim is applied, however, insert a notched handle as in **Diagram F**, making the notch lie on the top row of weaving so the rim fits in it.

Diagram F

22

Hearth Basket

This basket probably acquired its name from its use. It has been used in years past to carry wood, kindling maybe, and probably sat near or on the hearth. It makes an ideal carrier or magazine basket. Whatever its use, it is a lovely, serviceable basket.

APPROXIMATE SIZE
12" x 18" x 14"

MATERIALS NEEDED:
5/8" flat reed (weavers & stakes)
#6 round reed (rim)
3/16" flat reed (lashing)
12" x 14" D handle
#2 round reed (twining)
1/2" half round reed (optional runners)

PREPARING THE MATERIALS
Mark the halfway point on the bottom of the D handle in pencil. Select several of the heaviest strips of 5/8" flat reed. From these strips, cut 9 pieces 30" long and 8 pieces 25" long to be used as fillers. Then cut the following:

- 4 pieces 33"
- 4 pieces 30"
- 4 pieces 28"
- 2 pieces 26"

Determine the right and wrong side of the reed. The wrong side is the rougher, hairy side.

Measure and mark the halfway point on the wrong side of all these pieces. Place all the strips of reed in a container filled with warm water to soak 2 or 3 minutes.

WEAVING THE BOTTOM OF THE BASKET
On a table in front of you, place 5 of the 30" stakes horizontally, wrong side up. Place them so the outermost 2 are 12" apart (measuring from the outside edges). See **Diagram 1**.

Next, place the D handle on top (vertically) of the 5 strips, making sure it is exactly on the half-way mark on the reed. *Note:* If your handle happens to be a little wider or a little narrower than 12", simply adjust the 5 stakes by sliding them apart or pushing them in enough so that the outermost 2 are even with the outside edges of the handle.

Now, place the last four 30" stakes on top of the handle (horizontally, like the first 5), in the spaces between the first 5, wrong side up. Also, place the 25" pieces on each side of the four 30" pieces. See **Diagram 2**. *Note:* It is awkward to hold all these pieces in place until 2 or 3 rows are woven. A spoke weight or large book on one end of the horizontal stakes will help hold them in place.

The 25" filler pieces will be treated as one with the 30" pieces. Begin weaving across the base (vertically) with the longest (33") stakes. Weave 1 on each side of the handle. See **Diagram 3**. Continue to weave stakes in, alternating overs and unders in descending order, until all 14 pieces are in place. See **Diagram 4**. The left side of the base (not shown) is identical to the right.

Cut all the filler pieces as in **Diagram 5**, down the center of the stake to the edge of the woven base. Rewet the filler pieces if necessary. Bend them over and tuck them under the first available (vertically) woven stake. Half the split goes under a stake to the right

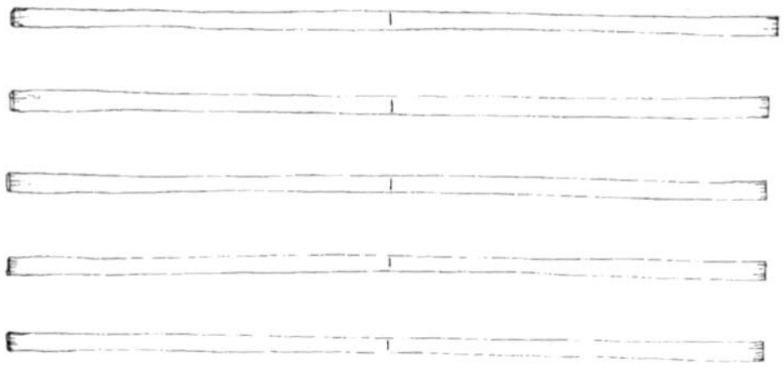

Diagram 1

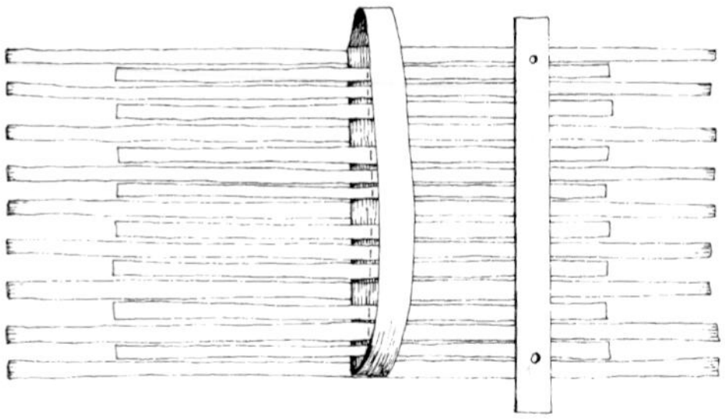

Diagram 2

and the other half to the left. See **Diagram 6**. Measure and true the base to 12" x 18". Mark in pencil the corners once the base is trued.

With a long soaked #2 round reed weaver, twine around the base as in **Diagram 7**. Begin by folding the weaver in half. Place the fold around any stake and twine around one row. End the twining by pushing the end under itself where it began.

WEAVING THE SIDES

Rewet the weavers if they are dry. To upsett the sides, bend each stake, vertical and horizontal, all the way over (to the inside) upon itself, forming a permanent crease at the base. Use ruler or piece of heavy cardboard as a guide for upsetting the sides. See **Diagram 8**.

Row 1: With a long, wet strip of 5/8" flat reed, begin weaving by placing the end of the strip on the inside of the handle and weaving over and under each stake. Weave all the way around the bas-

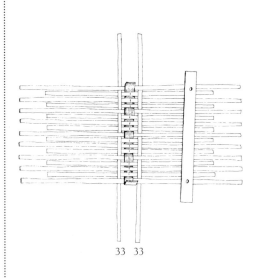

33   33

Diagram 3

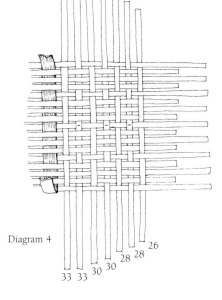

Diagram 4

33 33 30 30 28 28 26

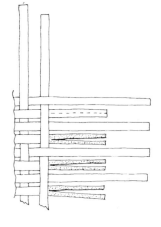

Diagram 5

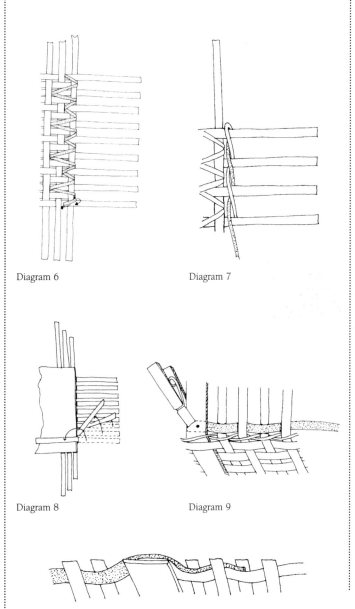

Diagram 6

Diagram 7

Diagram 8

Diagram 9

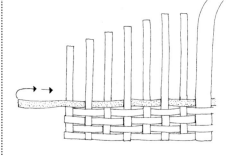

Diagram 10

ket, over 1, under 1, etc. See **Diagram 9**. Treat the handle as another stake. When you return to the starting point, allow the 2 ends to overlap 4 stakes before cutting. Make sure both ends are hidden. See **Diagram 10**. Each row is woven separately. Cut the weaver at an appropriate place.

Row 2: Begin another long weaver, on the opposite side of the basket, and weave over alternate stakes; in other words, "overs" of the last row will be "unders" on this row. Repeat the ending procedure.

Rows 3 & 4: Repeat rows 1 & 2, beginning the weavers at different spots than you started rows 1 and 2.

Row 5: From now on, you will work with the long sides of the basket one side at a time, relying on **Diagram 11**. Begin on either side with a new weaver, leaving about 4" free at the ends. When the row is all woven, wrap the 4" around the first and last stakes of the row, hiding the ends behind the

third stake. See **Diagram 12**.

Continue this procedure for 5 more rows, dropping in 1 stake every row. See **Diagram 13**.

Refer to **Diagram 14** for weaving the top row. The weaver begins on top of A and ends behind B. Weave the other side the same.

FINISHING THE STAKES
Soak a long piece of #2 round reed. Fold it nearly in half, loop the fold around a stake and twine around the basket for 3 rows. See **Diagram 15**. End twining by pushing ends under the twining where it began. Next, rewet the ends of the stakes if necessary, and after they have been pointed, bend them to the inside and tuck them behind the first available row of weaving. See **Diagram 16**.

Cut the edges of the stakes that extend beyond the twining parallel with the twining. See **Diagram 17**.

APPLYING THE RIM
Wrap a long, soaked piece of 5/8" flat reed all the way

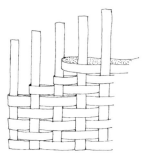

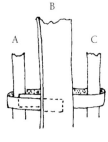

Diagram 11

Diagram 12

Diagram 13

Diagram 14

around the inside top edge of the basket, making a complete turn around the handle. Hold this strip in place with clothespins every 2" or 3". See **Diagram 18**. The wrong side of the reed should be against the basket. Overlap the ends about 2" and cut off the rest.

Now, wrap another strip of 5/8" reed around the outside top edge, making the same complete turn around the handle. Hold this strip in place with the same clothespins.

Lastly, place a piece of #6 round reed between the 2 pieces of flat reed. You will need 2 separate pieces, so the ends will butt against the handle on both sides. All 3 pieces are now held together with the clothespins. See **Diagram 19**.

Using a long piece of soaked 3/16" flat reed, flat oval reed or cane, lash all the 3 pieces together as in **Diagram 20**. Begin the lashing on the right-hand side of the handle so if there is any excess in the round reed, the lashing will ease it out the other end. Tuck the ends behind a stake so they are secure and won't pull out.

The corners can be squared by rewetting and pinching them or they can be left rounded, whichever you prefer.

The "runners" on the bottom of the basket are optional. Historically, they were used to give the basket a replaceable sitting surface and to keep the bottom from wearing. Measure the distance across the basket from edge to edge. Cut the 1/2" half round reed accordingly. Cut away half the thickness from the ends of the reed so they can be pushed under the outermost stakes as in **Diagram 21**.

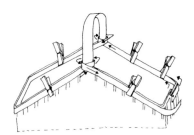

Diagram 18

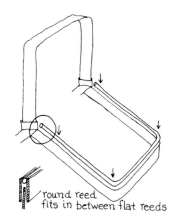

round reed fits in between flat reeds

Diagram 19

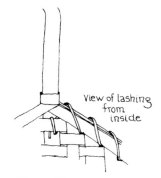

View of lashing from inside

Diagram 20

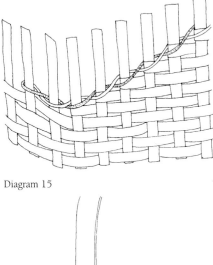

Diagram 15

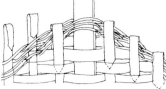

Diagram 16

---- cut off along this line

Diagram 17

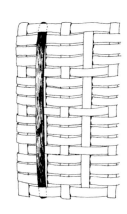

Diagram 21

Cherokee Market Basket

Thanks to Judith Olney of Rowley, Massachusetts, for sharing her directions for this basket with us. She found a picture of the basket in a book and worked out the pattern. The writer of the book termed it a Choctaw basket, but it lacked the typical Choctaw rim, so it seemed more probably an Eastern Cherokee.

BASE SIZE
12-1/2" x 15-3/4"

MATERIALS
1/4" flat or 7mm flat oval reed (stakes)
1/4" flat oval reed (weavers)
1/2" half round reed (rim)
3/16" flat reed (lashing)
3/8" flat reed (false weaver)
#3 seagrass (rim filler)
12" or 13" (span) square notched handle
Heavy cardboard or wood (mold)

PREPARATION
■ Dye 9 or 10 long pieces of 1/4" flat oval black.
■ Dye 8 or 9 long pieces of 1/4" flat oval red.
■ Dye the 3/16" flat reed for rim lashing red or black, or leave it natural.

Make a mold for your basket, if you wish, from heavy cardboard or wood that is 12-1/2" x 15-3/4" x 12" high. It is possible to make the basket without the mold, but it surely makes weaving much easier. A lightweight wood works well, as do pieces of heavy-duty cardboard taped together.

WEAVING THE BASE
From the 1/4" flat or 7mm flat oval, cut 54 pieces 37" long and 42 pieces 40" long. Soak all the pieces until they are pliable. Mark the centers on the wrong (rough) side of all the pieces. Lay 6 of the 40" pieces edge to edge horizontally. Mentally (or actually in pencil) number the pieces 1 to 6, with 1 being the closest to you. See **Diagram 1**.

Just to the right of the center marks, using the following pattern, weave in the first six 37" pieces. The center marks on these pieces should be just above horizontal piece #6:
■ #1 - under 4, 5 & 6; over 1, 2 & 3
■ #2 - under 1, 5 & 6; over 2, 3 & 4
■ #3 - under 1, 2 & 6; over 3, 4 & 5
■ #4 - under 1, 2 & 3; over 4, 5 & 6
■ #5 - under 2, 3 & 4; over 1, 5 & 6
■ #6 - under 3, 4 & 5; over 1, 2 & 6
See **Diagram 1**.

Continue to weave pieces to the right, repeating the weaving pattern until 27 pieces are in place. All rows are woven with edges flush together. Then weave the other 27 pieces to the left of the center mark following the established pattern. *Note:* You will reverse the weaving pattern—i.e., the first row to the left will be a repeat of row 6, then row 5, etc. The first row to the left of the center is shown in **Diagram 1**.

Next, weave the remaining 40" pieces horizontally, 21 pieces above the center mark and the remaining 15 below the first 6 that were positioned. These are all woven following the established pattern. *Note:* It is an over 3, under 3 twill pattern throughout. Once the base is all woven, measure and true it to 12-1/2" x 15-3/4". Measurement may vary slightly, since material sizes vary.

Place the mold (if you are using one) on the base. Tie the unwoven stakes up, making them stand and conform to the shape of the mold. Make the stakes stand straight and in the correct sequence. See **Diagram 2**. Allow the stakes to dry in

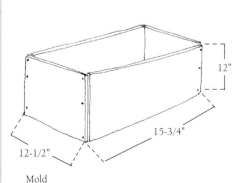

Mold

Diagram 1

1 2 3 4 5 6

place and do not rewet them unless they appear brittle and in danger of breaking. If you are not using a mold, upsett the stakes by bending them over on themselves toward the center of the base.

WEAVING THE SIDES

Soak several long pieces of natural 1/4" flat oval reed. Beginning in the middle of a long side and starting on the outside, weave over 3 stakes, one of which is a center stake of the side. Hold the weavers in place with clothespins. Continue around the basket weaving under 3, over 3, etc. See **Diagram 3**. End each row as in **Diagram 4**, overlapping to the next group of 3s.

Weave 6 rows of over 3, under 3 twill, stepping the pattern over 1 stake each row. See **Diagram 5**. Begin and end each row at a different place each time. Soak the dyed reed one piece at a time as you need it. Following the graph,

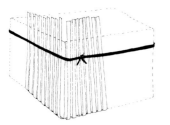

Diagram 2

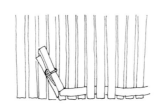

Diagram 3

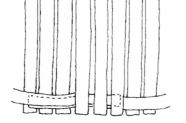

Diagram 4

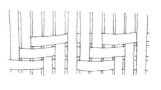

Diagram 5

Diagram 6, weave the first 5 pattern rows red, the next 9 rows black, and the last 5 rows red. Continue starting and stopping at a different spot each row. **Diagram 7** shows the last row of natural and the first 2 rows of color (pattern) woven.

Pack each row tightly against the previous row as it is completed. Finish weaving over 3, under 3, but not in a twill weave. Rather, weave in a plain weave, gradually pushing the stakes together and treating them as one. See **Diagram 8**. Weave 7 rows of natural 1/4" flat oval and finish with one row of 3/8" flat. Pack all rows one last time, dampen (if necessary) and tighten any rows that are loose,

especially at the corners.

FINISHING THE BASKET

Cut the groups of 3 that are on the inside of the basket flush with the top row of weaving. In the groups of 3 that are on the outside of the basket, cut 2 of the stakes flush with the top row of weaving, leaving the outermost one to be tucked to the inside. Point the remaining stake, rewet if it has dried and bend it to the inside of the basket, pushing it behind the first available row of weaving. See **Diagram 9**. Insert the handle into the weaving on the inside of the basket. Center the handle on each side and push the end behind only 2 or 3 rows so the notch is aligned with the

top row of weaving. See **Diagram 10**.

Measure the distance around the rim, allowing 2" or 3" to overlap. Soak the 1/2" half round reed thoroughly. Bevel the ends so the overlapped area is no thicker than a single thickness. Place one piece on the outside of the basket. Hold in place with clothespins.

Place another piece on the inside of the basket, allowing it to fall on the notch of the handle. The overlapped areas of the rim pieces should be near (within 2") of each other, but not at the same place. Hold

both pieces with heavy clothespins or clamps. Lay a piece of seagrass on top of and between the 2 rim pieces. Let the ends overlap for the moment. They can be cut later as the rim is lashed.

Starting just past the 2 overlapped areas, lash the rim pieces together as in **Diagram 11**. Push one end of a soaked 3/16" flat oval up between the rim pieces. Hook it over the basket wall and take the lasher into every space between spokes. When the starting point is reached, either end the lasher or reverse directions to "X" lash.

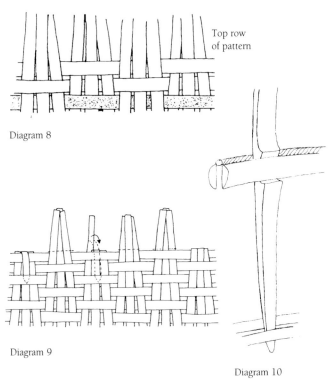

Top row
of pattern

Diagram 8

Diagram 9

Diagram 10

Diagram 6

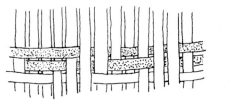

Diagram 7

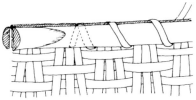

Diagram 11

Egg Basket

If there is any one basket that is truly representative of baskets made by early Americans, it must be the Appalachian egg basket, also known as a "gizzard" basket or "fanny" basket. It is a ribbed basket and, if care is given to certain details, not all that difficult to construct. There must be a hundred uses for the egg basket in your home while it's not carrying eggs, but if all else fails, hang it from your exposed beams.

APPROXIMATE SIZE
8" diameter x 8" high

MATERIALS
3/16" flat reed (weavers)
#6 round reed (ribs)
Two 8" round hoops
Waxed string

MEASURING & PREPARING THE HOOPS

The 8" egg basket requires a 12" exposed handle, which should be identified and marked first. Locate the splice (the point where the hoop has been joined in manufacturing) on the inside of one of the hoops. Holding the hoop with the splice in the bottom (or at 6 o'clock), place an identifying mark on the inside of the hoop in pencil. This will be the bottom of your handle hoop. Next, on the outside of the hoop, pencil a mark at 9 o'clock. With a tape measure on this mark, measure 12" around the top of the hoop and mark again on the outside. This second mark will be approximately at 3 o'clock. The marked area will become your basket's handle. See **Diagram 1**.

Next, make a mark 1/2" below the one at 9 o'clock. Do the same at 3 o'clock.

On the second, or rim, hoop, place the splice again at 6 o'clock. On the outside of the hoop, pencil a mark

across the width of the hoop at approximately 9 o'clock. From this mark, measure the circumference of the hoop. Divide the circumference in half and mark again on the outside of the hoop. This halfway mark should be at exactly 3 o'clock. From these marks, measure 1/2" clockwise and mark again. You now have marked 4 points at which the 2 hoops will intersect.

Slide the second, or rim, hoop through the first, or handle, hoop at a right angle, aligning the marks. See **Diagram 2**.

With a piece of waxed string, tie the 2 hoops together, making an X over both hoops. See **Diagram 3**.

Note: The handle hoop always goes on the outside of the rim hoop.

CUTTING THE RIBS

As you cut the ribs, number them in pencil. Place the numbers anywhere on the rib except the very end. See **Diagram 4**. From the #6 round reed, cut 2 each of the

following lengths: #I, 14"; #II, 15-1/2"; #III, 18"; #IV, 16-1/2"; #V, 14".

With a pencil sharpener or knife, sharpen all the ends of all the ribs. The #3 rib needs to be especially sharp. See **Diagram 4**. Place these ribs aside.

MAKING THE EAR

Identify the wrong and right side of the weavers. The wrong side has absolutely flat edges. The edges of the right side are slightly beveled or rounded.

Select a long (at least 8') weaver and soak it until it is pliable.

Begin the ear by placing the end of the weaver behind the intersecting point of the hoops, wrong side of weaver against the hoops, leaving about 1" free. Following the numbers in **Diagram 5** and starting at the dot, make an X over the intersecting hoops. Be sure to take the weaver over its tail when moving from 2 to 3.

Then, as in **Diagram 6**,

12"

9:00   3:00

splice

Diagram 1

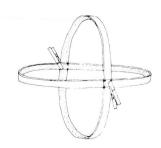

Diagram 2

Inside view

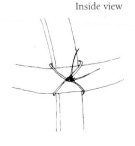

Diagram 3

begin the actual ear by bringing the weaver over the top of the handle hoop, up and around the right rim (6), down to (7) under the handle hoop and up to the left rim (8). Repeat, moving from one side to the other, keeping the wrong side of the weaver against the hoops, until you have 6 rows on both sides. Count the rows from the top of the rim. *Note:* If the loose end of the weaver (at dot) is in your way after the first revolution, secure it with the weaver, then cut it off. Make the ear as tight as possible.

The finished ear should look like **Diagram 7**. Do not cut the weaver. Secure it at the rim with a clothespin. Repeat the procedure on the other side.

INSERTING PRIMARY RIBS INTO EAR

The finished ear has 4 openings—1 underneath each rim (2) and 1 on either side of the bottom or handle hoop (2). Insert an awl into each of these spaces and move it around enough to open the space even more. See **Diagram 8**.

Now, insert the #1 ribs into the openings just underneath the rim, pushing and twisting at the same time

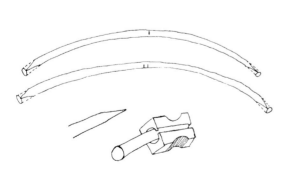

Diagram 4

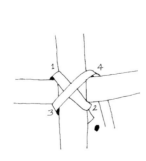

Diagram 5

Diagram 6

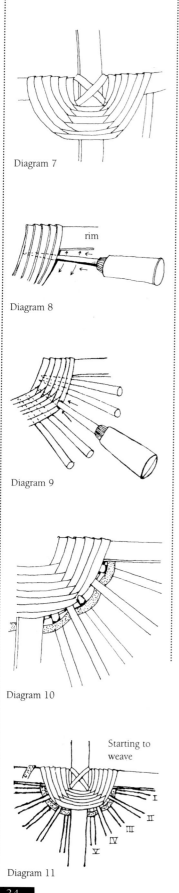

Diagram 7

Diagram 8

Diagram 9

Diagram 10

Starting to weave

Diagram 11

until they feel secure. Insert one on each side of the basket. Insert the #II ribs into the same space as #I, underneath #I.

Next, insert the #V ribs into the space on either side of the handle hoop (bottom of basket). Insert the #IV in the same space as, and above, the #V.

Last, referring to **Diagram 9**, make a hole in the reed between the #II and #IV ribs. This space was formed as a flat area when you made the ear. Move the awl back and forth to open up this space. The reed will actually split. Insert the #III rib in this opening on both sides. All the ribs are shown inserted in **Diagram 10**.

With all the primary ribs in place, the basic skeleton of the basket is formed. If the shape doesn't look right, adjust the ribs now, by lengthening or shortening as needed.

With the remainder of the weaver secured at the rim, bring the weaver behind the rim, over rib #I, under #II, over #III, etc., until you reach the other side. See **Diagram 11** for beginning to weave. Rewet the weaver anytime that it feels dry and/or stiff. *Note:* If the ribs "pop out" just put

them back in and continue to weave. You must make the weavers fit in as closely as possible to the ear.

Weave 5 rows as in **Diagram 12**. When a weaver runs out, add a new one, referring to **Diagram 13**. Lay the new wet weaver on top of the old one. Weave with both the old and new weavers until the old one runs out, then continue to weave with the new one.

PREPARING & INSERTING SECONDARY RIBS

Again, from the #6 round reed, cut 2 each of the following ribs: #1, 12"; #2, 14"; #4, 15"; #5, 13".
Note: These measurements are approximate and may need adjusting slightly.

The secondary ribs are inserted into the basket in the following places: #1 above #I; #2 above #II; #4 below #IV; #5 below #V.

The secondary ribs are inserted beside a primary rib with the point reaching only under the first available weaver, not all the way into the ear. See **Diagram 14**. Don't hesitate to add more if you need them. A good rule of thumb is that if you can get 2 fingers between any 2 ribs, you need to add another rib.

FINISHING THE BASKET

Because of the shape of the egg basket, the rim and the bottom of the handle hoop will fill with weavers before the fullest areas do, leaving a football-shaped area unwoven. See **Diagram 15**. As you weave, push the weaving on the rim and on the handle hoop outward toward the ears as much as you can. This will allow room for more weavers. When you can no longer squeeze in another weaver, turn around a rib and weave in the opposite direction. See **Diagram 16**. *Note:* For the sake of clarity, the finished diagram shows more space between weaving than directed. The actual weaving should be tighter. There is an alternate means of filling in unwoven space after 10 or 15 rows are woven on each side: Fold a long soaked weaver in half over the rim, wrong side against the rim. See **Diagram 17**. Use clothespins frequently to keep the ribs evenly spaced. You are now weaving with 1 end of the weaver at a time, 1 end toward the left and 1 end toward the right. When this weaving covers 5" or 6" of the rim, stop weaving and return to the original weaving

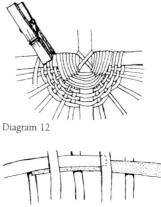

Diagram 12

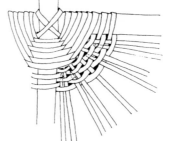

Diagram 13

Diagram 14

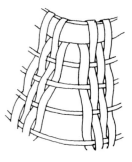

Diagram 15

on the sides. When the 2 areas meet, you should fill in the triangular unwoven space. When you can no longer squeeze another weaver in around the rim, do one of the following:

1. Turn around the first rib, reversing the direction just as you did around the rim. See **Diagram 18**.

2. Cut the weaver inside the basket and begin a new one going in the opposite direction. See **Diagram 19**.

If your finished basket doesn't sit level, rewet the weavers and ribs and place a heavy object in the side that isn't level. Allow the basket to dry with the object in it.

MULTICOLORED EGG BASKET

To make the multicolored fanny basket pictured on the cover, you'll need: 10" x 15" oval hoop (rim), 10" round hoop (handle), #0 and #1 round reed dyed in several colors (weavers), fine cane dyed 1 of the colors (weavers), #7 round reed (ribs), 3/16" flat reed dyed (God's Eye).

Following the directions for the egg basket, use the round hoop for the rim and the oval hoop for the handle. The exposed handle is 18".

Construct the God's Eye, following the directions for the melon basket. Make at least 8 revolutions around the hoops. Cut the weaver and tuck the end under the wraps on the inside on one of the rims.

Cut the following ribs from the #7 round reed: #1, 29"; #2, 27"; #3, 28"; #4, 19"; #5, 24"; #6, 23"; #7, 26"; #8, 27"; #9, 13"; #10, 14-1/2"; #11, 20"; #12, 21"; #13, 18"; #14, 20"; #15, 23"; #16, 23"; #17, 23"; #18, 23".

Taper all the ribs for about 2", on one side only, making them almost paper thin at the very end.

Insert ribs 1, 2 and 3 as in **Diagram A**. Weave around the 3 ribs, over and under, for 36 rows (counting each row from one rim to the other), changing colors as desired.

Start and stop rows between ribs 1 and 2.

Add the next 5 ribs as in **Diagram A**, pushing them under several rows of weaving. Resume weaving for 16 rows. Add the other 10 ribs as in **Diagram B**. Resume weaving with the dyed cane, wrong side out, for 15 rows. Again resume weaving with the round reed. Each row, weave 2 rows all the way around the rim. On each row thereafter, turn around every other rib, beginning with the first or second, then the third or fourth, etc. This helps keep a straight line of weaving around the basket and fill in the football-shaped area as you go.

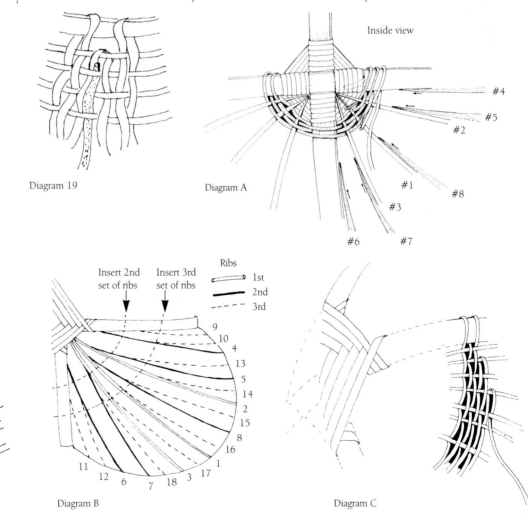

Diagram 16

Diagram 17

Diagram 18

Diagram 19

Diagram A

Inside view

#4

#5

#2

#1

#8

#3

#6

#7

Diagram B

Insert 2nd set of ribs

Insert 3rd set of ribs

Ribs
1st
2nd
3rd

9
10
4
13
5
14
2
15
8
16
1
11
12   6   7   18   3   17

Diagram C

35

Double Chief's Daughter Urn

The woven pattern in this basket is, of course, Cherokee in origin. Used mostly as a floor basket, it is wonderful anywhere you use it.

APPROXIMATE SIZE
10" x 10" x 15" high

MATERIALS NEEDED
1/4" flat reed (stakes and weavers)
#0 round reed (locking row)
3/8" flat oval reed (rim)

PRELIMINARY STEP

Dye approximately 1/3 hank of 1/4" flat reed rust, or the color of your choice. Also dye 2 long pieces dark brown or black.

WEAVING THE BASE

From the natural 1/4" flat reed, cut 72 pieces 50" long. Mark the centers of all the pieces on the wrong side. Soak all the pieces until they are pliable.

Lay 36 pieces horizontally in front of you, wrong side up, aligning center marks. Use a spoke weight or heavy book to hold them in place.

Weave 2 pieces vertically through the horizontal pieces just to the right of the center marks, as in **Diagram 1**. Beginning at the bottom, weave over 4, under 4, etc., with 2 pieces. Place the center mark of the vertical piece in the center of the 36 horizontal pieces.

Continue to weave with 2 pieces in the following pattern (Row 1 is already woven):
Row 2: u2, o4, u4, o4, etc., ending with o2.
Row 3: u4, o4, u4, etc.
Row 4: o2, u4, o4, u4, etc.

Repeat these 4 rows until 18 pieces are woven in to the right of the center mark.

Next, weave the other 18 pieces to the left of the center mark, again repeating the following 4-row pattern:
Row 1: o2, u4, o4, u4, etc.
Row 2: u4, o4, u4, o4, etc.
Row 3: u2, o4, u4, o4, etc.
Row 4: o4, u4, o4, u4, etc.
Row 5 will be a repeat of Row 1.

Diagram 2 shows 4 rows woven to the right of the center mark and 4 rows woven to the left.

Measure and true the base to 10" x 10". Mark the corners of the base when it is trued in case any slipping occurs.

All rows should fit flush against each other as snugly as possible. Pack and repack, as some shrinking will occur when the reed dries.

The next step is optional. If you foresee a need for a locking row, twine around the base with #0 round reed to hold everything in place while you begin weaving up the sides. Fold a soaked piece of #0 round reed in half, loop the fold around any set of two stakes and twine around the base as in **Diagram 3**. End the twining by tucking the end under itself where it began.

The twining can be removed later (after the sides are well on their way up) if you wish.

WEAVING THE SIDES

Note: From the bottom of the basket, the order of color and natural woven up the sides is as follows:
Row 1-6: Natural.
Row 7-33: Rust.
Row 34-41: Natural.

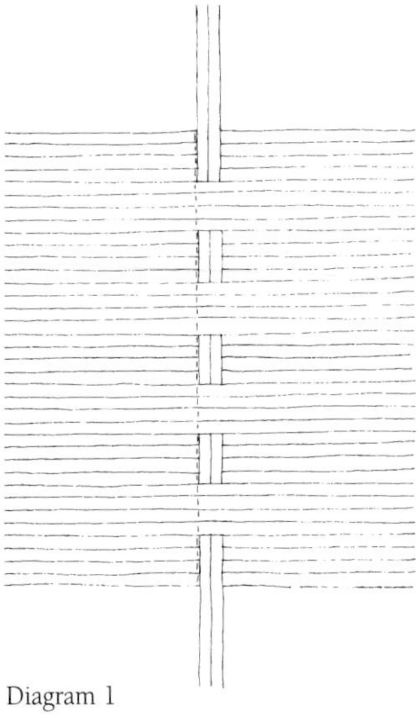

Diagram 1

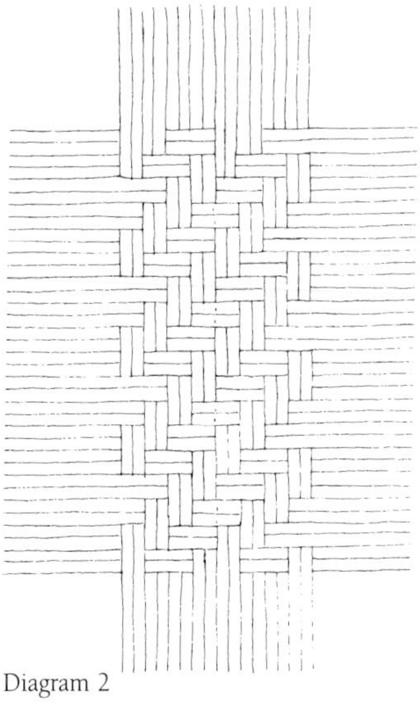

Diagram 2

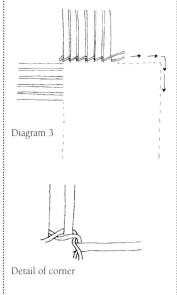

Diagram 3

Detail of corner

Row 42: Black.
Row 43: Rust.
Row 44: Black.
Row 45-53: Natural.

Starting anywhere with a soaked 1/4" flat reed, weave over 4, under 4 around the basket. See **Diagram 4**. Be sure the right side of the weaver is on the outside. Cut the weaver after it has overlapped the beginning, and hide the end behind the fourth group of stakes. See **Diagram 5**.

Weave 6 rows in this same manner, making the "over 4" move over two stakes each row. See **Diagram 6**.

When 6 rows are done, soak several pieces of rust 1/4" reed. To locate a starting place, count from the right corner (any side) to the ninth stake. Looking at **Diagram 7**, place the end of the weaver over the ninth, tenth, eleventh, twelfth and thirteenth

stakes. Go under the next 3, over 1, under 3, etc., following the graph in **Diagram 8**.

Diagram 9 shows the second row begun.

Be sure to start each row on a different side from the row before.

Continue following the graph through Row 33. Pack each row down tightly against the previous row.

WEAVING THE NECK
Row 34 (natural) is over 3, under 3. Locate an "o5" on the last pattern row. Take the weaver under the center 3, over the next 3, under the next 3, etc.

Row 35 (natural) is also over 3, under 3, but opposite the row before (not twilled) as are the rest of the rows. Begin on this row to pull the 3 stakes you are weaving over (or under) together as in

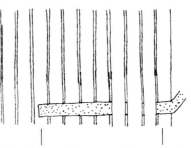

9th stake from right   Front corner long side

Diagram 7

Diagram 8

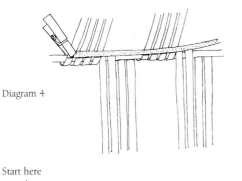

Diagram 4

Start here

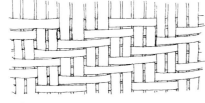

Diagram 5   End here

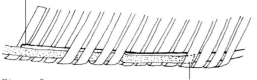

Diagram 6

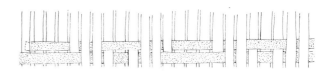

Diagram 9

Diagram 10, treating them as one. They must be pushed together to allow space for the weaver to fit in.

Also, after Row 35, start to pull tightly on the weavers to restrict the diameter of the neck. The diameter should decrease about 2" by time the 8 natural rows are done.

Next, weave in a black weaver, still pulling tightly on the weaver. The next row is a rust weaver and then another black one. See **Diagram 11**.

Now you must make the stakes flare outward. Try, if you want, to control the flare by weaving from the inside of the basket and pressing outward on the stakes. If you have trouble getting them to flare, soak the ends of the stakes and turn the basket

upside down, making the stakes spread out drastically. See **Diagram 12**. Place some heavy object on the bottom (now on top) so the stakes are pressed outward as far as possible—far more exaggerated than you eventually want them. They will invariably pull in some as you weave.

Weave over 1 (treating 3 stakes as one) under 1 until you are within 2" of the ends of the stakes.

FINISHING

When you are within 2" of the ends of the stakes, looking at **Diagram 13**, cut off the stakes on the *outside* of the basket flush with the top row of weaving. One of the 3 stakes on the *inside* of the basket gets tucked into the weaving on the *outside* of the basket and the other 2 in the group are cut flush with the top row of weaving.

Soak a long piece of 3/8" flat oval reed. Measure around the top rim of the basket. Allow enough for a 3" overlap, cut and bevel the ends for 3" so the thickness of the overlap is no thicker than a single thickness of 3/8" flat oval. Place 1 piece around the rim on the inside and 1 on the outside, covering just the last row of weaving and holding them in place with clothespins. Place the overlapped areas near, but not on top of each other. Begin lashing just past the 2 overlaps as in **Diagram 14**. Hook the lasher over the basket wall going under the inside rim, then lash around the rim pieces, taking the lasher in each space between every 3 stakes. End the lasher as you began or hide it behind the top row of weaving.

Diagram 12

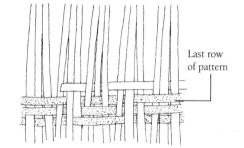

Last row of pattern

Diagram 10

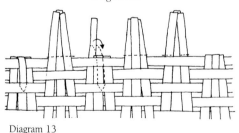

Diagram 13

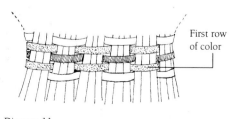

First row of color

Diagram 11

Diagram 14

Shaker Cheese Basket

The Shaker cheese basket is, historically, just what its name implies. It was used in the Shaker community in the cheese-making process. It is used today to adorn the walls, mantles and tables of many Primitive and Early American homes. It is not difficult to make and is certainly a wonderful accent piece. Thanks to Janet Finger of Willmar, Minnesota, for her instructions and basket.

APPROXIMATE SIZE
8" diameter x 13" high

MATERIALS
1/4" flat reed (heavy for stakes)
1/4" flat reed (lighter weight for weaving and lashing)
1/2" flat oval reed (rim)
5/8" half round reed (handle)

The directions given here will produce a 7-hole basket. The size can be increased or decreased as you choose, but you must always have an uneven number of holes. To determine the number of strips you will need to make the base, add one to the number of holes you want and multiply by 3. Thus, for a 7 hole basket you will need 24 strips (7 + 1 = 8 x 3 = 24).

From the heaviest 1/4" flat reed, cut 24 pieces 30" long. Soak all the pieces until they are pliable. Mark the centers of all the pieces on the wrong side in pencil.

Following **Diagram 1**, place 2 strips of 1/4" flat reed horizontally in front of you, wrong side up, laying them about 1" apart.

Note: The entire base will be laid with the wrong side up.

Holding them in your hand, cross 2 more pieces at their center marks with the right one over the left. From now on, the one you have held in your right hand and have placed over the other piece will be considered the "right diagonal" piece. Place the X you have formed on top of the 2 horizontal pieces just to the left of the center marks, tucking the ends of the right hand piece under the horizontal strips as shown.

Now make another X the same way and place it to the right of the first X, again tucking the right diagonal under the top horizontal

piece. Where the ends of the horizontals intersect they will be locked in place. Being "locked" means to have the right diagonal over the left diagonal. See **Diagram 2**. This locking is extremely important and is the fundamental thing to remember when doing hexagonal weaving. You should now have one little hexagon in the center of the two X's, shown by the dotted lines in **Diagram 2**.

Continue adding X's on either side of the original until you have 7 X's, 3 on each side of the original hexagon. Take time now to even everything, making sure you have 7 little hexagons of the same size reasonably centered on your 2 long horizontal strips. Also, make sure that all the left diagonals are locked under the right diagonals. See **Diagram 3**.

Now the weaving becomes easier. Take another soaked strip and weave it

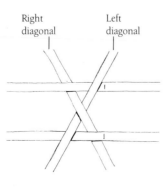

Right diagonal   Left diagonal

Left diagonal locked under right

Diagram 1   Diagram 2

horizontally through the upper 7 X's, over the right diagonals and under the left. Again, lock everything in place and even the hexagons. The first new piece is woven in **Diagram 4** and can be identified by the shading. Take another soaked strip and weave it above the previous one, through the upper section of the 6 X's. Make sure all the ends are locked. Repeat this step once more, and you will have 5 horizontal strips with 7 hexagons between the first 2 horizontal strips that were laid and 4 at the top under the last horizontal strip that was woven. **Diagram 4** shows the entire top half of the basket.

Now you must make the lower half of the base look like the top. Some find it easier to turn the entire base around and repeat what you just did, weaving 3 more horizontal rows above the original ones. The completed

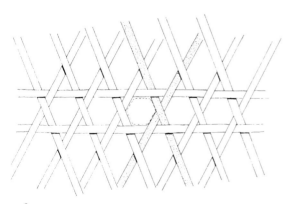

Diagram 3

Diagram 4

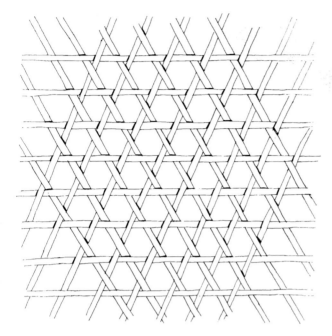

Diagram 5

Diagram 6

Diagram 7

base should look like **Diagram 5**. Check carefully to see that everything is locked in place and the base itself is a hexagon. The base should measure approximately 9" at its widest point and 4-1/2" on each of the 6 sides. The more perfectly shaped the hexagonal base, the easier it will be to bring the side up evenly. Notice that around the base, there are 4 X's on each of the 6 sides. These are the X's you will use to weave up the sides.

WEAVING THE SIDES

Soak several pieces of 1/4" flat reed for weavers. Also, resoak the base if it has dried. Gently bend the reed upwards at the edge of the base. It is not meant to stand straight up at this point or to be creased, simply nudged upward.

Hold the base in front of you with the bottom (right side of the reed) closest to you. Tuck the end of a soaked weaver behind the stake farthest to the left on any side, right side out. Weave just as you wove the base horizontals, under the

left diagonal and over the right. Lock each newly formed X as you come to it. Use clothespins to help hold everything in place. If you have problems with this, say out loud to yourself, "Under the left one, over the right one, lock. Under, over, lock." You should be gently forcing the sides up away from you during this process. When you reach the first corner, the last left diagonal upright on a side is locked in by the first right diagonal upright on the next side. It will feel strange and the hexagon formed will look less than perfect too, but this is normal. See **Diagram 6**.

When you have woven around all 6 sides, overlap the beginning of the weaver for 2 or 3 X's and hide the end behind either a stake or itself. See **Diagram 7**. Ask yourself the following questions: 1. Are all the diagonals locked? 2. Are the hexagons evenly shaped and approximately the same size as the base hexagons? 3. Are the sides fairly upright? Row 2 should make the sides absolutely upright and row 1

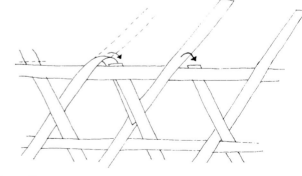

Diagram 8

can always be adjusted later. Add 5 more rows of weaving in the same manner you wove row 1, starting and stopping each row in a different place.

FINISHING THE STAKES & APPLYING THE RIM & HANDLE

Soak the entire basket and straighten everything, again making sure the hexagons are truly hexagonal. Cut all the inside uprights (the right diagonals) flush with the top row. Fold the outside uprights (the left diagonals) over and push them behind the X below and to the right. See **Diagram 8**. Trim each stake as you go.

Soak two pieces of 1/2" flat oval reed, each long enough to reach around the rim of the basket twice and overlap 3". Measure the exact amount of overlap by holding the rim in place with clothespins and marking the overlapped area. Remove it from the basket and shave half the thickness from the top of one side and half the thickness from the bottom of the other side where the two will overlap. Replace the rim

pieces, placing the overlapped areas near but not on top of each other. Hold both the pieces in place with clothespins. With a long soaked piece of 1/4" flat reed, begin lashing as in **Diagram 9** by hooking the end of the lasher over the top row of weaving from the inside to the outside of the basket. Continue to lash with the long piece of reed by going into each hole under the rim, around the rim and into the next space. End the lasher as it began or by pushing the end down behind one of the X's inside the basket.

To make the handle, soak a piece of 5/8" half round reed that is 33" long. Soak it until it is pliable, then shave the rounded side on each end for 9" until it becomes about 3/16" thick. See **Diagram 10**. Use a knife or a trimming plane to thin the half round reed. Carefully narrow the ends with a knife so they are no wider than 1/4" for the last 1-1/2". Bend the handle into the shape you want. On both ends of the handle, drill holes at 8"

and 9", using either an awl or a power drill. See **Diagram 11**. Immediately, push the 1/4" ends through the holes from inside to outside to inside, looping the ends through a space in the side of the basket. See **Diagram 12**. Be sure to choose 2 spaces that are directly across the basket from each other when putting the handle in place. Use a heavy rubber band or string to make the handle stay in the shape you want until it dries.

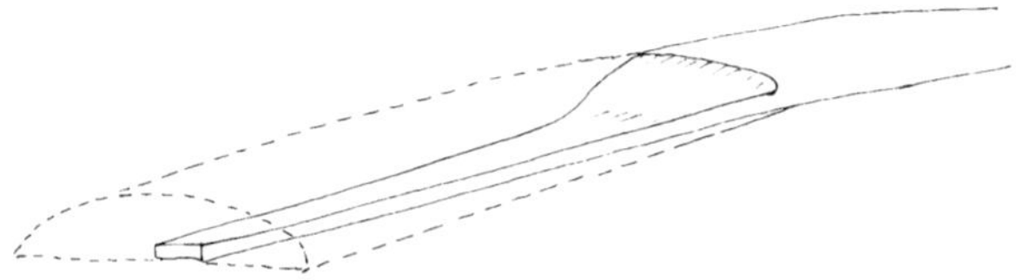

Diagram 10

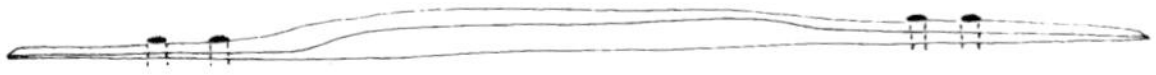

Diagram 11

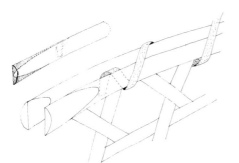

Diagram 9

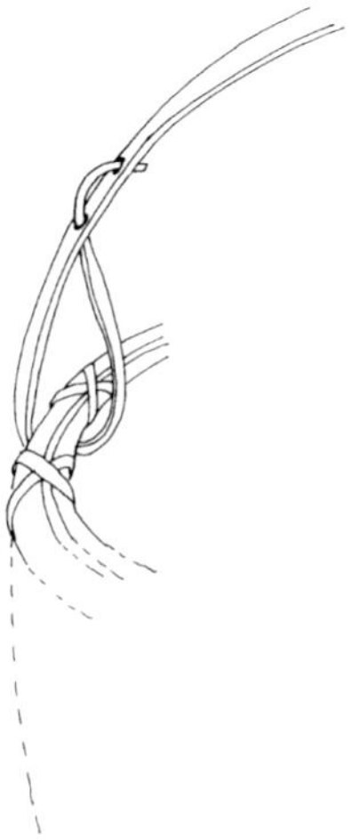

Diagram 12

Bean Pot

A reproduction of an old basket that was made in Pennsylvania, of rye straw, the bean pot is a popular beginner's basket. Particularly nice hanging by its wire handle, it can decorate a hearth or tabletop as well. Other handles can be substituted, of course, as shown in the photograph.

APPROXIMATE SIZE

9" top diameter x 7" high

MATERIALS NEEDED

1 bean pot handle with eyelets
1/2" flat reed (spokes)
#2 round reed (twining)
1/4" flat oval reed (weavers & lashing)
1/2" flat oval reed (rim)
#2 or #3 seagrass (rim filler)
3/8" flat reed (1 piece for false weaver)

TWINING THE BASE

From the 1/2" flat reed, cut 12 pieces 27" long. Soak all the pieces until they are pliable. In pencil, mark the centers of all the pieces on the wrong side. Also in pencil, mark 1-1/2" on each side of the center mark of 6 pieces.

Lay the 6 pieces with the 1-1/2" marks, as in **Diagram 1**, like spokes in a wheel. Soak a long piece of #2 round reed until it is pliable. Fold it a little off center and begin twining as in **Diagram 2**, by looping the fold around one of the bottom spokes and taking the top piece under the next spoke.

Add on to the ends of each piece if necessary, as in **Diagram 3**, by tucking the old end beside a spoke and adding a new one beside the spoke before.

When the diameter of the twined area is about 6" or when there is ample room for a new spoke, lay the other 6 spokes in the spaces between existing spokes as you come to them. See **Diagram 4**. Continue twining around all 12 spokes. When the diameter of the whole base is 7" to 7-1/2", end the twining as in **Diagram 5**, by tucking the ends of the reed into the twined area beside a spoke.

WEAVING THE SIDES

Soak a long piece of 1/4" flat oval reed and taper one end for about 4", so that the first inch is only about 1/8" wide. Cut one spoke in half lengthwise. Upsett all the spokes by bending them over toward the center of the base.

Begin weaving with the tapered weaver by pushing the tapered end between the 2 pieces you created by cutting the spoke. Weave over and under the spokes around the base and continue another round when the starting point is reached. See **Diagram 6**.

Note: By cutting the spoke in half, you have created an odd number of spokes so a continuous weave can be done.

Do not make the spokes stand straight, but rather let them lean outward to increase the diameter of the basket. Add on to the weaver when one runs out as in **Diagram 7**. Slip the new weaver behind a spoke with

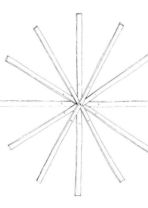

Diagram 1

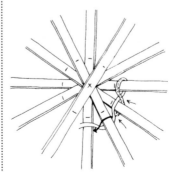

Diagram 2

Diagram 3

the old one and continue with both until the old one runs out. After 10 to 12 rows of weaving have been done, the diameter of the basket should be approximately 10" to 11", its widest point. From this point on, apply more tension on the weaver and press in on the spokes to make the diameter decrease to approximately 9" (after approximately 27 rows) at the top opening of the basket.

The shape of the basket should resemble **Diagram 8**. To end the weaving, taper the weaver for about 4", again making the last inch no wider than 1/8" wide. End the weaver directly above the beginning point. See **Diagram 9**.

FINISHING THE BASKET

Soak the piece of 3/8" flat reed. Locate the 2 pieces you cut in half. Bring them together as closely as possible and weave over them as one

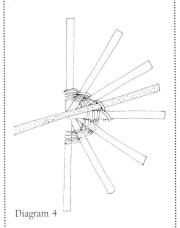

Diagram 4

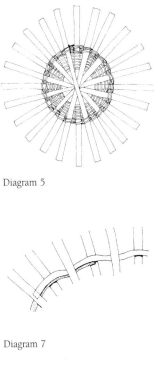

Diagram 5

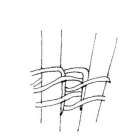

Detail of Diagram 5

Diagram 7

Diagram 8

Diagram 6

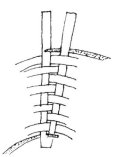

Diagram 9

spoke. Weave 1 start-stop row with the 3/8" flat reed, overlapping the ends for 4 spokes. See **Diagram 10**.

Cut all the spokes that are on the inside of the basket flush with the top row of weaving. Point and tuck all the spokes that are on the outside of the basket. Tuck the spokes behind the first available row of weaving on the inside of the basket. See **Diagram 11**.

APPLYING THE RIM AND HANDLE

Soak a piece of 1/2" flat oval reed that is long enough to reach around the top of the basket 2 times plus 6" to 8" overlap. Place the 1/2" flat oval reed (rim) around the outside of the basket, covering only the row of 3/8" flat reed. Overlap the ends 2" to 3". Hold in place with clothespins. Mark the reed where the overlap occurs.

Remove the rim and, with a knife or plane, bevel the ends so the overlapped area is no thicker than a single thickness of 1/2" flat oval. Repeat the procedure on the inside of the basket. See **Diagram 12**.

Reposition the 2 rim pieces on the basket after the ends are shaved. Place the splices (overlapped areas) near, but not exactly opposite, each other. Again, hold both pieces in place with clothespins. Locate any 2 spokes that are directly across from each other. Curve the eyelets to fit the shape of the rim. Push the ends under a bent and tucked spoke. Make sure the eyelet is directly above the center spoke. See **Diagram 13**.

Lay a piece of seagrass on top of and between the 2 rim pieces. Let the ends overlap for the moment.

They can be cut later as the rim is lashed. Starting just past the 2 overlapped areas, lash the rim pieces together as in **Diagram 14**. Push one end of a soaked 1/4" flat oval reed up between the 2 rim pieces. Hook it over the basket wall to secure it, and take the lasher into every space between spokes. When the starting point is reached, either end the lasher or reverse directions to "X" lash. End the same way you began, by hooking the lasher over the wall, or hide the end behind a weaver inside the basket.

With needle nose pliers, bend the ends of the handle as in **Diagram 15** and slip them through the eyelets. Tighten the ends of the handle around the eyelets with the pliers so it cannot slip out.

Diagram 10

Diagram 12

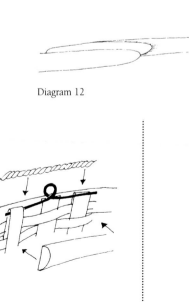
Diagram 14

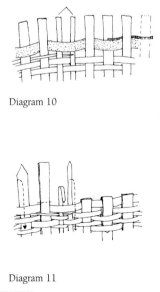
Diagram 11

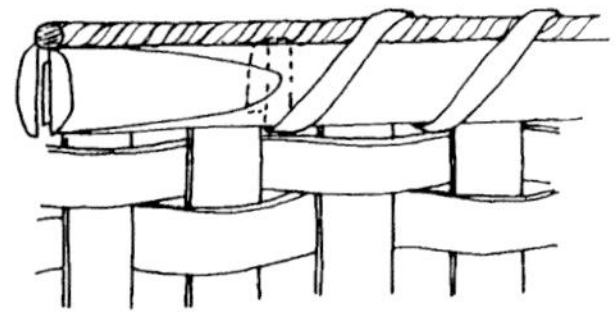

Diagram 13

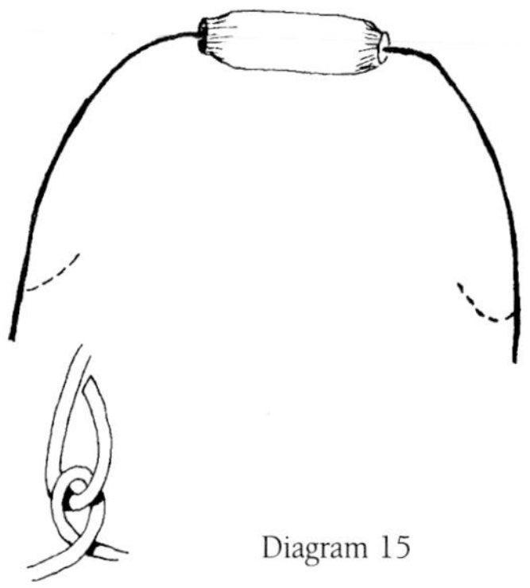

Diagram 15

EUROPEAN COUNTRY

2

Pine Needle Garden Basket

Many thanks to my special friend, Larry Walther of Clyde, North Carolina. For those who aspire to make baskets from pine needles, Larry's instructions are most clear and his style is certainly worthy of emulation. In case you don't have a ready source for pine needles, addresses of suppliers are listed at the end of the book. This wonderful basket can be used or just displayed, if you wish, as you would any other objet d'art.

APPROXIMATE SIZE
12" diameter x 9" high

MATERIALS AND TOOLS
8 oz. longleaf pine needles
1-1/4" diameter plastic ring
72" of 18 gauge wire
4-ply cotton candlewicking
   thread (color of your
   choice)
Manicuring scissors
Beeswax
#19 tapestry needle
Straight pins or washable felt
   tip pen

PREPARATION
Trim the pine needles just beyond the sheath. Any dust or pitch must be removed by washing in a mild detergent, rinsing in clear water and drying thoroughly. If you want to dye the needles, use a large stove-top pan. Bring 2" of water to a boil. Mix in 1 package of household or basketry dye and reduce it to a simmer. Put in up to 1/2 pound of pine needles. Simmer until the desired shade is reached, usually 3 to 5 minutes. Rinse well and dry thoroughly before using. Pastel colors are not usually successful because of the relatively dark shade of the needles. Colors such as brown, denim, rust, dark green and mauve are the most effective.

MAKING THE CENTER
Begin by folding a 48" length of waxed thread and placing the fold through the plastic ring. See **Diagram 1**. Pass the ends through the loop, creating a lark's head knot. Draw snug. See **Diagram 2**.

Hold the ring with the left hand and position the knot on the right outside edge of the ring. Spread the tails so the upper one (A) crosses the ring to the left and the lower one (B) is free and to the right. See **Diagram 3**. Take the lower tail (B) and lay the end below the knot and across in front of the plastic ring, forming a loop out to the right. Thread the end through the plastic ring, around and up through the loop just formed. Pull the tail snugly and slide the loop upward to form a tiny knot on the outside surface of the plastic ring. See **Diagram 4**.

Bring the left tail (A) up through the center of the plastic ring below the tail and slide the loop to the right around the plastic ring until it is snugly against the loop created by tail (B). See **Diagram 5**. The result will be a tiny knot on the inside surface of the plastic ring. See **Diagram 6**.

Continue around the plastic ring by repeating first the B loop and then the A loop, pulling each snugly against the other until the ring is completely covered. **Diagram 7**. The tails should be kept separate when tightening the loops. All the B loops will form a ridge on the outside surface of the ring and the A loops will form a ridge on the inside surface of the ring. The front and back surfaces of the ring should be smooth and free of knots.

When the ring is completely covered, rotate it a 1/4 turn counterclockwise and thread the B tail, as in **Diagram 8**, on the tapestry needle. Pierce the beginning or

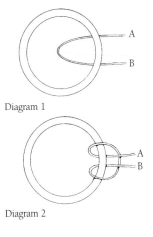

Diagram 1

Diagram 2

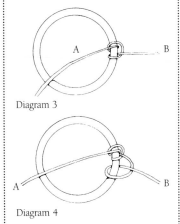

Diagram 3

Diagram 4

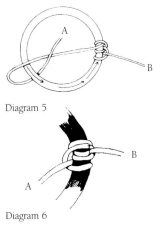

Diagram 5

Diagram 6

first outside knot and stitch over and under the next few knots (a running stitch). Remove the thread from the needle but do not cut it off. If you have at least 15" of thread A left, you may start filling in the spiderweb pattern. If not, secure the thread by stitching through a few more knots. Snip it off and start a new thread using the same method.

There are 12 spokes in the spiderweb pattern. Now, looking at **Diagram 9**, think of a clock face. Thread A through the needle and repeat the running stitch on the inside row of knots at 12 o'clock and go down to 6 o'clock. This is shown in **Diagram 9**. Weave your needle up and down through the buttonhole stitches on the left of the 6 and come up through the 7. Cross the center and come down through the 1. Stitch through to the right and come up through the 2. Cross the center again and go down through the 8. Continue in this manner, connecting the 9 with the 3, the 4 with the 10 and the 11 with the 5. The 12 spokes are now completed. See **Diagram 10**.

Finish by returning to the center from the 5 o'clock

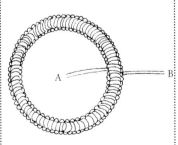

Diagram 7

Diagram 8

Diagram 9

Diagram 10

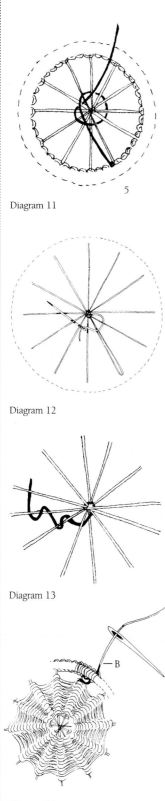

Diagram 11

Diagram 12

Diagram 13

Diagram 14

position on the ring. The thread will parallel the last completed spoke. This double spoke will be covered in the weaving process, explained in the next step. Tie an overhand knot in the middle where all the spokes converge. See **Diagram 11**.

You are now ready to fill in the spiderweb pattern. Begin by inserting the needle down between any 2 spokes, as in **Diagram 12**. Come back up 2 spokes to the left. Pull snugly. Go down again 1 spoke to the right and come up 2 spokes to the left. **Diagram 13** shows the pattern you will establish. Continue around the wheel in a clockwise direction until the entire ring is filled. Stitch through a few more of the buttonhole stitches and snip off the tail end of the thread on the back of the ring.

The beginning disk around which the basket will be constructed is now complete. If you still have at least 15" of thread on the outside of the

ring from tail B, you may use it to attach the first of the pine needles, as in **Diagram 14**. If not, add a new strand as previously described. Be sure to wax your thread each time you rethread your needle. This will prevent knotting or snarling and helps ease the thread through the work.

BEGINNING THE PINE NEEDLE COIL

Since the first few coils wrap around a disk that is only 1-1/4" in diameter, they must be flexible. Dampen a few dozen pine needles by soaking them in water for a few minutes and blotting them dry of excess moisture. Select 6 or 7 of varying lengths with the tapered ends facing in one direction and stagger them to avoid having a blunt end. Looking at **Diagram 15**, hold the completed disk with the finished side up. Lay the pine needles on the outside surface of the disk with the blunt ends to the left. Bring the threaded needle around the pine needle

coil, overcasting from front to back and come up in a buttonhole stitch slightly to the left of where the sewing thread begins. You will need 3 stitches for every spoke in the disk, for a total of 36 stitches. If you spaced your spokes consistently, this should be relatively easy. By the time you are halfway around the disk, you should have 18 stitches and the pine needle coil should be firmly attached.

As the coil comes around, as in **Diagram 16**, work the loose ends of the pine needles that were left protruding at the beginning under this first coil. This will bring you back to the first stitch. Bring the sewing needle up through the center of the coil and pierce the first stitch, then the next, as in **Diagram 17**. This is called a chain stitch and will be used until the basket bottom is completed. Continue this stitch until another 6 or 8 have been pierced. It is now time to start adding more pine needles.

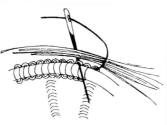

Take 3 stitches between each spoke, on outside of ring

Diagram 15

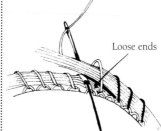

Loose ends

Diagram 16

Diagram 17

From this point on, pine needles will be inserted into the coil blunt end first. See **Diagram 18**. Determine how thick you want the coil to be. A 1/4" diameter coil is the most attractive in a basket of this size. With every stitch or two, slide another pine needle into the coil (blunt end first) until the desired coil thickness is achieved. Face the smooth, shiny surface of the pine needle to the outside of the coil. New thread may be added by back stitching over a few stitches. See **Diagram 19**. Continue stitching and adding pine needles until the basket bottom reaches 6" in diameter. At this point, the piece will be 18" in circumference and your stitches will be about 1/2" apart. The result will be a spiral pattern curving to the left. See **Diagram 20**. Colors may be introduced into the weaving at your discretion. Concentric bands of 2 colors with a band of natural separating them are most effective. When starting a new

color, do not slip them into the coil as usual, but lay them one by one on the outside edge of the coil until the previous color has been completely stitched over. Then they may be fed into the coil as before.

The floor of the basket is now completed. See **Diagram 21**. Using straight pins or a washable felt tip pen, divide the outer edge of the disk into 4 equal parts. Two opposite pins will represent the center of the raised sides and the other 2 will represent the center of the 2 low sides. As the basket grows, the stitches will become too far apart to keep it rigid. To avoid this, it is necessary to double the number of stitches. To do this, push the sewing needle twice through each stitch in the final row, as in **Diagram 22**. Work completely around once more until you have 72 stitches, which should resemble 36 V's. Continue this pattern, stitching a V inside each previous V. Note that this results

in an attractive pattern on the reverse side of the basket, which will become exposed as the basket builds up.

Continue stitching, rolling the sides at a sharp angle and the ends only slightly. **Diagram 23** shows these angles. This will result in an oval shape. Work until the oval shape reaches a length of 11" The width at this point will be approximately 9". Resting on a flat surface, the ends should be about 3/4" high and sides about 2" high. Your last stitch should be in the center of one of the low sides. See **Diagram 24**.

MAKING THE HANDLE

At this point, remove the 4 straight pins and reposition them on the outer edge and in the center of each long side and each short side. Measure and make sure that they are equidistant from each other. Measure the distance around the basket and cut 2 pieces of the 18 gauge wire 1" longer than the circumference.

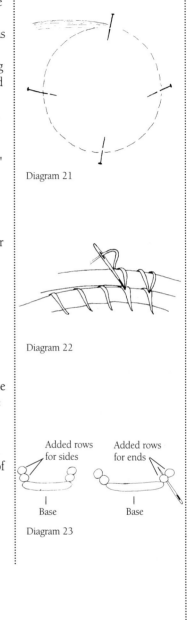

Diagram 21

Diagram 22

Added rows for sides   Added rows for ends

Base   Base

Diagram 23

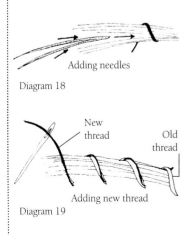

Adding needles

Diagram 18

New thread   Old thread

Adding new thread

Diagram 19

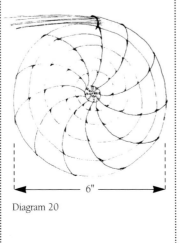

6"

Diagram 20

3/4"

Diagram 24

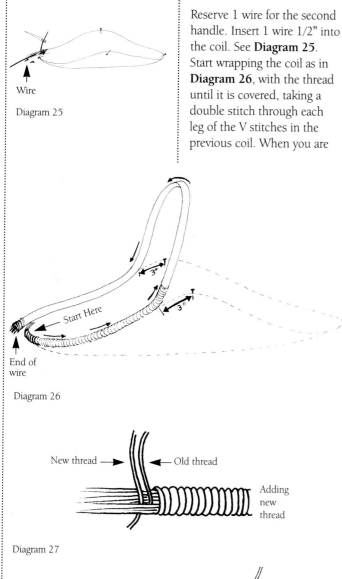

Wire

Diagram 25

Start Here

End of wire

Diagram 26

New thread ———→ ←——— Old thread

Adding new thread

Diagram 27

Reserve 1 wire for the second handle. Insert 1 wire 1/2" into the coil. See **Diagram 25**. Start wrapping the coil as in **Diagram 26**, with the thread until it is covered, taking a double stitch through each leg of the V stitches in the previous coil. When you are

3" short of the first side pin, double stitch into the previous coil and remove your needle from the thread. Continue wrapping and adding pine needles until only 1" or 2" of thread remains. Pull the end of the thread through the center of the coil and lay a new thread next to it. See **Diagram 27**. Continue wrapping, laying both ends next to the coil and wrapping over them. Add new thread as needed.

When you have wrapped enough of the handle to reach a point 3" beyond the opposite side pin, stitch twice to the previous coil. There should be enough of the wire core handle to reach 1/2" past the starting point. The wire core must be a complete circle to lend strength to the handle. Continue wrapping and stitching until the wrapped coil meets itself.

Revert to the V stitch and complete 1 more coil around the wrapped coil, spacing the stitches about 1/2" apart as in

Diagram 28. Now reverse your stitching direction and go backward, passing the needle through the same hole each time, as in **Diagram 29**. End near the center of the low side.

Using the second piece of 18 gauge wire and 6 or 7 pine needles, start a second handle in the center of the opposite low side. **Diagram 30** shows how the handle begins gradually so that there is a smooth transition from the rim to the handle. Stitch a little way to secure the ends and then start wrapping. Duplicate what you did with the first handle. Bend the 2 handles upward until they rest against each other. Pin them together and then stitch them to each other starting at a point approximately 3-1/2" above the high sides of the basket, as in **Diagram 31**. The wire core will render the handle flexible enough to shape it easily. The finished handle should be about 9-1/2" high.

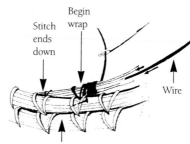

End view

Diagram 28

First do 1 row of vee stitches, then reverse and back stitch on the same hole

Diagram 29

Stitch ends down

Begin wrap

Wire

Center of end

Diagram 30

3-1/2"

Side view

Diagram 31

An exceptionally sturdy basket because of the double bottom and double walls, this one can really be used. Gather herbs or flowers in it and later hang it from a beam or set it on a hearth, full of baby's breath, to decorate your home.

APPROXIMATE SIZE OVERALL
12" x 15" x 16"high

MATERIALS NEEDED
5/8" flat reed (spokes)
1/2" flat reed (spokes)
1/4" flat oval reed (weavers
   and lashing)
5/8" ash, poplar or maple
   (weaver)
#2 round reed (twining)
1/2" flat oval reed (rim)
#2 seagrass (rim filler)
10" swing handle with ears
Navy dye

Oval Double Wall

PRELIMINARY STEP
Dye approximately 14 yards of 1/2" flat reed, approximately 1/3 hank of 1/4" flat oval reed and 10 to 12 long pieces of #2 round reed, either navy or the color of your choice.

PREPARING MATERIALS & WEAVING THE BASE
From the dyed 1/2" reed, cut 16 pieces 26" long. From the natural 5/8" flat reed, cut 16 pieces 26" long. Soak all the pieces along with several long pieces of #2 round reed.

Mark the center of all the 5/8" pieces on the *rough* sides. Mark the 1/2" pieces on the *smooth* sides. Place the 1/2" pieces on top of the 5/8" pieces, *wrong sides together,* and treat them as one for now. Consider holding the 2 pieces together with a clothespin or paper clip. On one piece make pencil marks 2-1/4" on each side of the center mark, and on another piece mark 1-1/4" on each side of the center mark.

Lay the piece with 2-1/4" marks vertically and lay the one with 1-1/4" marks perpendicular to the first, matching center marks as in **Diagram 1**. The four marks will act as a general guide for the oval base.

Lay 6 more pieces, alternating directions as in **Diagram 2**. With all 8 pieces in place, fold a long piece of dyed #2 round reed almost in half and begin twining on one of the marks. See **Diagram 3** for how to twine. *Note:* If you can squeeze the

twining closer to the center than 1-1/4", it will make the oval even more defined. All the time you are twining, keep packing the twined rows toward the center, keeping the base as oval as possible.

To add a weaver when twining, add on to each end as it runs out as in **Diagram 4**. Twine around the 6 spokes until the base measures 6" or 7" x 8" or 9", or until there is ample room in the spaces between spokes for another spoke.

Continue twining and lay the other 8 spokes in the spaces as you come to them. See **Diagram 5** for adding the first new spoke. Lay the others in the same manner. Twine around all 16 spokes until the base measures approximately 8" x 10". End the twining as in **Diagram 6**.

UPSETTING THE SPOKES & WEAVING THE SIDES
Dampen the dyed spokes and bend them over upon themselves, forming a permanent

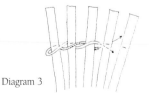

Diagram 3

Diagram 1

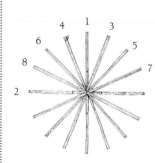

Diagram 2

Diagram 4

crease at the base. The base should resemble **Diagram 7** at this point. Soak a long piece of dyed 1/4" flat oval reed and begin weaving in start-stop fashion. See **Diagram 8** for how to begin and end a row. Overlap the ends for 4 spokes. Place the oval side of the weaver on the *inside* of the basket.

Note: If the reed is very thick and the overlapping will cause too much bulk, shave some of the thickness from the oval side, being careful that the shaved area will not show from the inside of the basket.

Weave 28 start-stop rows, beginning each row at a different place so as not to create a build-up. Make every effort to flare the sides. **Diagram 9** shows 4 rows woven on the inside wall.

Next, dampen the 5/8" (natural) spokes and bend them up, leaning them against the already woven inside wall. Again, weave start-stop rows

Diagram 5

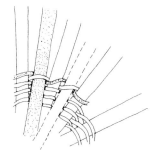

Diagram 6

with soaked natural 1/4" flat oval reed, turning the oval side now to the *outside* of the basket. See **Diagram 10**. Again, shave some of the thickness from the oval side of the reed at the overlap to avoid too much bulk.

Note: Make sure each spoke lies directly on top of the one already standing. At the top of the basket, the two are again treated as one. Weave:

- ■ 12 rows of 1/4" flat oval (natural)
- ■ 1 row of 1/4" navy flat oval
- ■ 1 row of natural 5/8" ash
- ■ 1 row of navy 1/4" flat oval

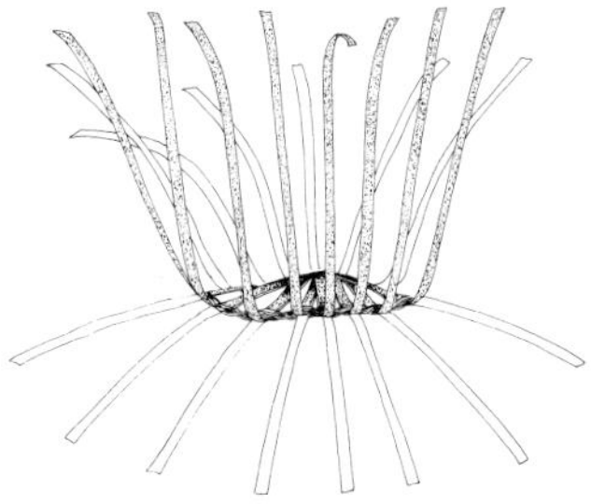

Diagram 7

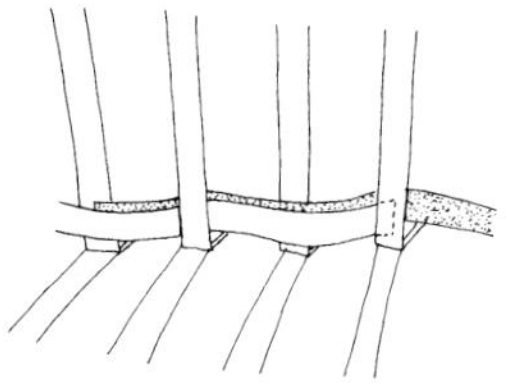

Diagram 8

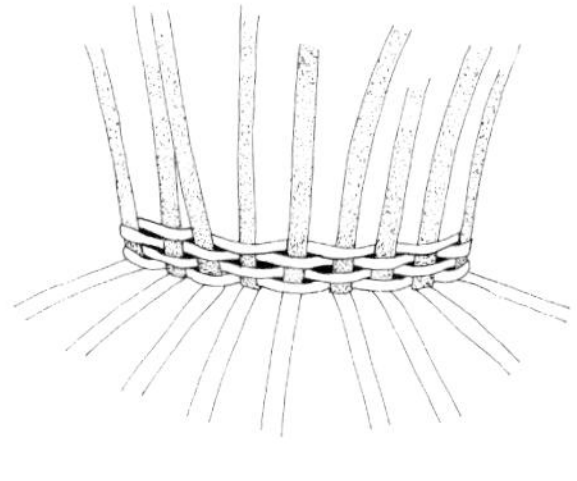

Diagram 9

- ■ 12 rows of 1/4" flat oval (natural)

See **Diagram 11** for woven rows. Keep the outside wall pressed very close to the inside wall all the time it is being woven.

If, when you finish, the 2 walls are not exactly the same height, try packing the taller one down to conform with the other. If necessary, weave an extra row or take one out on either wall to make the 2 the same height.

FINISHING THE BASKET

With a long soaked #2 round reed, twine around the spokes as in **Diagram 12** for 3 rows. End the twining directly above the starting point by

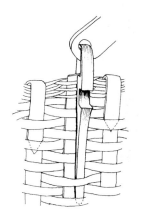

Diagram 10

Diagram 11

Diagram 12

pushing the reed down into the twined area beside a spoke. Cut all the outside natural spokes flush with the top row of twining. Point the inside (dyed) spokes and push them over the twining and to the inside, hiding the ends behind the first available weaver. See **Diagram 13**.

Insert the ears (with handle attached) into the weaving on the outside and the inside of the basket as in **Diagrams 13** and **14**. Make the notches fall on the rows of twining so the rim will fit into them. Soak 2 pieces of 1/2 flat oval reed, each long enough to reach around the rim of the basket and overlap for 3".

Place 1 piece on the inside

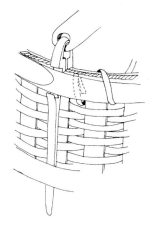

Diagram 13

Diagram 14

rim and the other on the out-side. Measure and mark the area of overlap. Remove the 1/2" flat oval from the basket and, with a knife or plane, bevel the ends of both pieces so the overlapped area is no thicker than a single thickness of 1/2" flat oval reed. See **Diagram 15**.

Replace on basket, holding in place with clothespins. Place a piece of seagrass between the 2 rim pieces so the end of the spokes are covered.

Lash the rim pieces in place with a long soaked piece of 1/4" flat oval reed as in **Diagram 14**. Begin by pushing the lasher up between the rim pieces and "hooking" it over the basket wall to secure it. Continue by bringing it up behind, around the front and into the space between spokes. Take the lasher between all the spokes and end the same as it began. Wet and reshape the basket if necessary. Use a heavy rubber band if needed. Place around the sides and allow it to dry in place to achieve a more oval shape.

Lastly, lash a "foot" in place by using a long soaked piece of 1/4" flat oval, either natural or navy. Begin by slid-ing one end under a row of twining about 3" from the center of the base. Continue moving around the base, tak-ing the weaver under the twining at every spoke. When the starting point is reached, reverse the direction and make an X over the last row. See **Diagram 16**. **Diagram 17** shows the foot on the bottom of the basket.

Diagram 15   Diagram 16   Diagram 17

Ribbons & Roses

Make this little basket over a glass bowl so it can hold potpourri, candy or whatever you like. You may use any size glass bowl and perhaps increase the size of your reed as the size of the bowl increases. Ours was 3" deep, 5-1/2" in diameter at the top opening and approximately 3" in diameter at the base. Any bowl of approximately the same size will work fine. Thanks to Patti Hill of Weaverville, North Carolina, for her help in designing this basket.

APPROXIMATE SIZE

6" deep X 4" high

MATERIALS NEEDED

#3 round reed (spokes)
#1 round reed (weavers)
11/64" flat reed dyed the
    color of your choice
    (weavers)
36" of 1/2" ribbon to match
    dyed reed (rose)
2 pieces of #2 round reed
    dyed the same as the
    11/64" flat reed
Bowl
Needle and thread

MAKING THE BASE

Cut 16 pieces of #3 round reed 30" long. Mark the centers of all the pieces and soak them until they are pliable. Lay them as in **Diagram 1**, in groups of 4, over the base of the bowl. With a long soaked #1 round reed weaver, begin weaving around the base also as in **Diagram 1**, starting the tail of the weaver over A. Weave over 1 group, under the next, etc., around the 8 groups for 3 rows.

After 3 rows, turn around 1 group to reverse directions, and make 3 rows in the other direction as well. The weaver will be going over and under opposite groups. After the second 3 rows, split the spokes in pairs as in **Diagram 2**, adding a new soaked weaver by pushing the end under the woven area. The 2 spokes in a pair will be treated as 1 spoke from now on. With two weavers you must weave and chase. The weaver farthest ahead moves all the way around the base going over 1 and under 1. When it catches up with the other weaver, drop the first one, and with the second one (the chaser), weave opposite overs and unders until it catches up with the first. Continue alternating weaver and chaser for 6 rows, or until you have reached the edge of the base of the bowl just before the sides. End

the 2 weavers by pushing the ends into the weaving beside a spoke. See **Diagram 3**. *Note:* Should you need more assistance with the weave and chase method, see "Up Close and Technical."

As in **Diagram 4**, start 3 new weavers behind any 3 consecutive spokes, and make 1 row of 3-rod wale. The farthest left weaver moves over 2 spokes and behind the third each stroke.

As in **Diagram 5**, end one of the weavers being used for 3-rod wale behind its starting spoke. Resume weaving and chasing with the remaining 2 weavers. Should you need to add on a new weaver, do so as in **Diagram 6**, by tucking the old end to the right of a spoke and starting a new one in the weaving on the right of the spoke before.

Note: All the time you are weaving, you must hold the base in place on the bowl and make sure it conforms to the shape of the bowl. The tighter

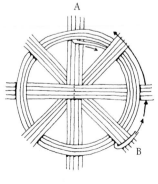

Diagram 1

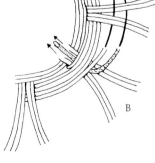

Diagram 2

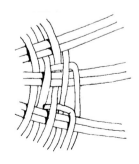

Diagram 3

you weave in the beginning, the better it conforms.

WEAVING THE SIDES

When you have woven approximately 10 rows of weave-chase, end the weavers as before. Now, weave 8 rows of start-stop weave with the 11/64" flat dyed reed. See **Diagram 7** for how to start and stop rows. Always end behind a spoke so the end doesn't show from the outside.

Next, weave in the ribbon and tie the bow. See **Diagram 8**. Weave 1 more row of dyed 11/64" flat oval reed in start-stop weaving. With a long piece of soaked #1 round reed, resume weaving and chasing by folding the weaver around any spoke. See **Diagram 9**. Weave and chase for 16 rows or until the top edge of the bowl is reached. End the 2 weavers as before.

MAKING THE BORDER

This border will hold the bowl in place. It cannot be removed once the border is made. Soak the ends of the spokes and, as in **Diagram 10**, bend each spoke (pair) over to the right, behind the spoke to its right to the outside. If you mark the beginning spoke it is easily identified later. Move around the basket, taking each spoke behind the next and to the outside. End by lifting the first spoke and pushing the last one behind it and out. See **Diagram 11**.

Starting anywhere, take each spoke over the one to the right and to the inside. See **Diagram 12**. End as before, lifting the first spoke and pushing the end through. See **Diagram 13**.

Again start anywhere and, as in **Diagram 14**, on the inside of the basket, take any spoke to the right under 1, over the next and down, making it lie against the inside wall of the bowl. The last one will end just as before by going under the

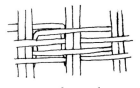

View from inside

Diagram 6

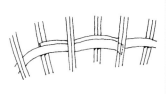

Diagram 7

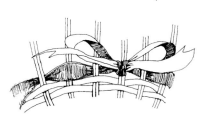

Diagram 8

Diagram 9

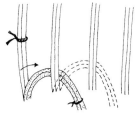

Diagram 10

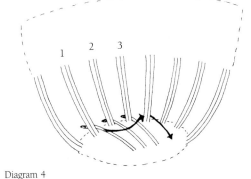

Diagram 4

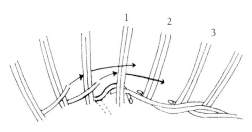

Diagram 5

Diagram 11

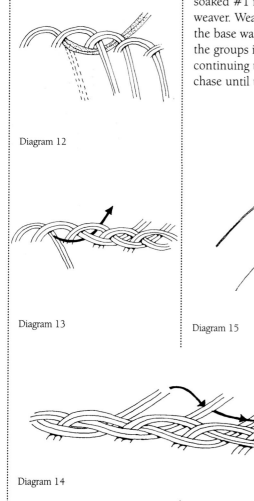

Diagram 12

Diagram 13

Diagram 14

beginning spoke, over the next and down. Leave the ends until they are dry. Then cut them at an angle that doesn't show from the top.

MAKING THE LID

Cut 16 pieces of #3 round reed 12" long. Soak them and mark the centers. Lay them as in **Diagram 1** and begin weaving with a long soaked #1 round reed weaver. Weave the same as the base was woven, splitting the groups into pairs and continuing to weave and chase until the diameter is

about 4". End the #1 round reed weavers. Begin 2 pieces of dyed #2 round reed, and weave and chase for 6 rows, or until the diameter of the top is about 1/2" smaller than the top of the bowl. The border will be about 1/2" wide. End the colored weavers by tucking the ends into the weaving beside 2 spokes.

To make the border of the lid, repeat steps 1 and 2 of the basket border. Looking at **Diagrams 10, 11** and **12**, take any spoke under 1 to the right to the outside. End

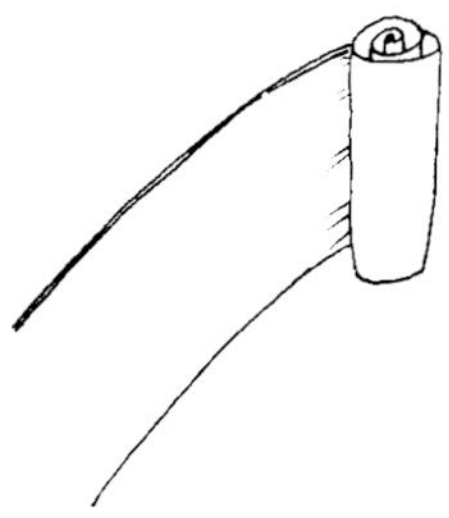

Diagram 15

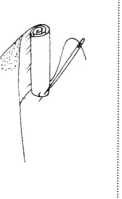

Diagram 16

Diagram 17

the row as previously described. Next, starting anywhere, take each spoke over the one to its right to the inside. Let spokes dry in place and cut on the inside of the lid.

MAKING THE RIBBON ROSE

To form the center of the rose, roll one end of the ribbon 5 or 6 times around to make a tight roll. See **Diagram 15**. Sew a few stitches at the base of the roll with matching thread, just to hold it tight. See **Diagram 16**.

To form the petals, fold

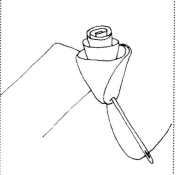

Diagram 18

Diagram 19

the top edge of the un-
wound ribbon down toward
you so it is parallel to the
roll and the folded edge is at
a 45 degree angle. See **Diagram 17**.

Use the sewn base of the
roll as a pivot point and roll
the flower across the fold,
making it very loose at the
top and tight at the base.
Make small tacking stitches
every revolution. See **Diagrams 18** and **19**. Petals can
be made by stitching the sel-
vage edges together as in
Diagram 20. Stitch ends
together and sew through
with a running stitch to gather the piece in the center. See
Diagrams 21 and **22**.

Place the rose on the
petal and stitch in place.

Roses can be sewn
through the lid or glued in
place. See **Diagram 23**.

Diagram 20

Diagram 21

Diagram 22

Diagram 23

Willow Field Basket

Many thanks to Kris Aymar of Glenwood, Maryland, for this great gathering basket. Make it from willow if you can or from round reed. Large enough to hold children's toys, large dried flowers or lots of magazines, it can be very functional as well as decorative in your home. A special feature of the basket is a detachable "foot" that can be replaced when it wears. It is optional and the basket is complete without it.

APPROXIMATE SIZE

Overall 17" diameter x 13" high

MATERIALS

#7 round reed (spokes)
#5 round reed (weavers)
#10 round reed (handles)
#3 round reed (handle wrap)

WEAVING THE BASE

From the #7 round reed, cut 8 pieces 11" long and 32 pieces 44" long. Mark the centers of the 8 pieces and lay them as in **Diagram 1**, 4 pieces over 4 pieces, with center marks aligned. Soak a long piece of #5 round reed until it is pliable. Fold it almost in half. Loop the fold around one of the 4 sets of spokes. Take the top piece under the next group and the bottom piece to the top. Continue around the base with the weavers alternating overs and unders around the 4 groups 2 times.

After 2 revolutions, split the groups into pairs. See **Diagram 2**. After twining 2 or 3 more revolutions around the pairs, split them into singles and continue to twine around each single spoke.

Twine around the spokes until the diameter of the base is 9".

When a weaver ends, add a new one as in **Diagram 3**. End the old piece behind a spoke and lay the new piece beside it on the same spoke, overlapping the 2 for approximately 1".

When the base is 9" across, tuck the ends of the twining into the weaving beside any 2 consecutive spokes. See **Diagram 4**. Point the 32 spokes and push them into the weaving, one on each side of an existing spoke, for about 2".

Cut the ends of the original 8 spokes evenly with the last row of twining. See **Diagram 5**.

Turn the base over and, using the 32 added spokes, start 3 long pieces of #5 round reed behind 3 consecutive spokes and make 2 rows of 3-rod wale. The farthest left weaver moves over 2 spokes, to the right, over 2 spokes, behind 1 and out to the front. Always pick up the farthest left weaver. See **Diagram 6**.

Pinch the spokes with needle nose pliers so they will upsett easier and without breaking.

WEAVING THE SIDES

Upsett the spokes and cut 2 of the weavers that were used to make the 3-rod wale. Using the 1 remaining weaver, weave over 1, under 1 for

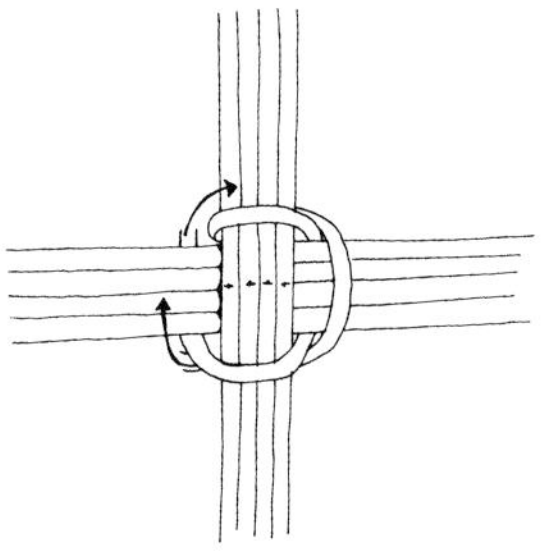

Diagram 1

Diagram 2

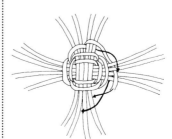

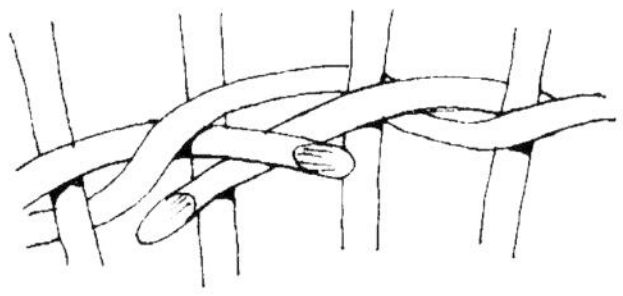

Diagram 3

32 rows. When the first spoke of each round is reached after each revolution, the weaver must go over 2 spokes so as to put it in an alternate "over-under" path. Every row will end with the "over 2," which will move over 1 spoke each row, creating a spiral design. In 32 rows the spiral will make 1 complete revolution around the basket. See **Diagram 7**.

Stop after 32 rows behind the spoke where you began. Add 2 long soaked #5 weavers behind the next 2 spokes and do 2 rows of 3-rod wale as before. Stop the 3 weavers, start 1 long soaked weaver and return to the over 1, under 1, but weave in the opposite direction from the other for 32 rows.

Again you must weave over 2 at the end of each row. The "over 2" will spiral in the opposite direction from the other spiral.

After 32 rows are done, add 2 soaked weavers again and work 1 row of 3-rod

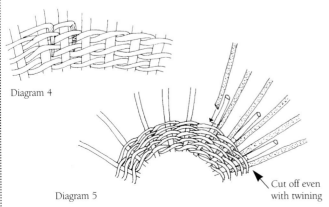

Diagram 4

Diagram 5

Cut off even
with twining

Diagram 6

Diagram 7

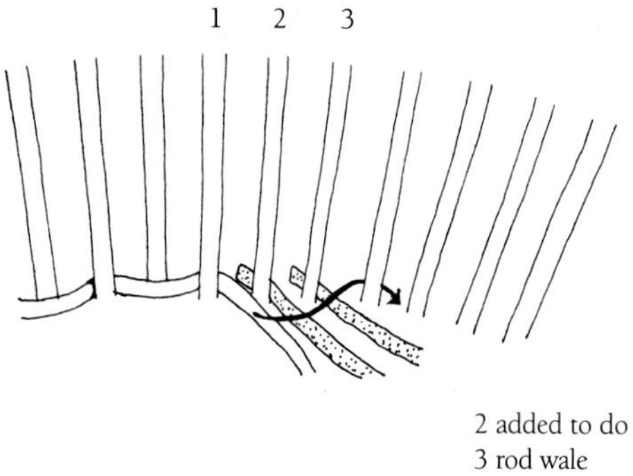

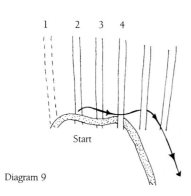

1 2 3

2 added to do
3 rod wale

Diagram 8

1 2 3 4

Start

Diagram 9

wale. See **Diagram 8**. Stop the row by ending the 3 weavers behind the spokes on which they began.

MAKING THE BORDER

Soak the ends of the spokes until they are pliable again.

Take each spoke in turn to the right in front of 2 spokes, behind 1 spoke and back out to the outside. See **Diagram 9**. **Diagram 10** shows 3 spokes already in place and the arrow demonstrates the path the fourth spoke should take. **Diagram 11** illustrates how the last 2 spokes are woven. The last spoke goes under the first 2 spokes that were positioned.

With all the spokes on the outside, starting anywhere, take each spoke over the 2 spokes to its right and to the inside, going under the loose ends, as in **Diagram 12**. Let the spokes lie

against the inside wall of the basket. Cut them close to the border when dry.

MAKING THE HANDLES

Cut 2 pieces of #10 round reed, each about 15" long. Soak them until they are very pliable. Bend them into the shape you want and allow them to dry in place. When dry, taper the ends and push them into the weaving with 2 spokes, leaving 2 spokes between.

Soak a long piece of #3 round reed and begin wrapping as in **Diagram 13**, by pushing the end of the weaver into the woven area on the side of the basket to secure it. Starting on the left of the handle, bring the wrapping over the border and around the handle, as in **Diagram 13**. Make 3 wraps around the handle and then around the border again and make the

Row 1

1 2 3 4

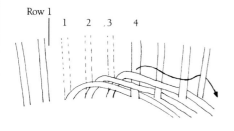

Diagram 10

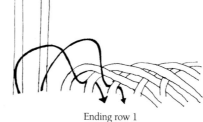

Ending row 1

Diagram 11

Lift up

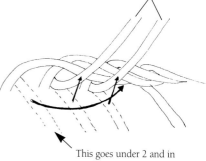

This goes under 2 and in

Diagram 12

second wrap in the opposite direction. Continue to wrap in first one direction and then the other until all the space is filled in. See **Diagram 14**. Should a weaver run out before the wrapping is done, add a new one as in **Diagram 15**, bringing it from the inside to the outside. The end of the new weaver is pushed into the weaving on the left of the handle.

When the handle is solidly wrapped, soak another weaver of the same size, push the end into the weaving and bind the handle wrap just above the border for 3 to 5 wraps, as in **Diagram 16**, with the aid of an awl. End the weaver by pushing the tail down into the binding.

MAKING THE FOOT
Turn the basket upside down and, using the pieces that remain from cutting the spokes (12" long at least), slype the ends and insert them about 2" into the weaving beside every other spoke. You will be inserting the new pieces from the base into the sides of the basket. See **Diagram 17**. Soak 3 long pieces of #5 round reed. Still holding the basket upside down, start them behind any 3 consecutive spokes. Work 1 row of 3-rod wale around the new spokes as previously described. End the row of waling as before, behind the starting spokes. See **Diagram 18**. With the remaining spokes, repeat the border made on the top of the basket. Refer to **Diagrams 9, 10, 11** and **12**. This foot can be removed and replaced if necessary.

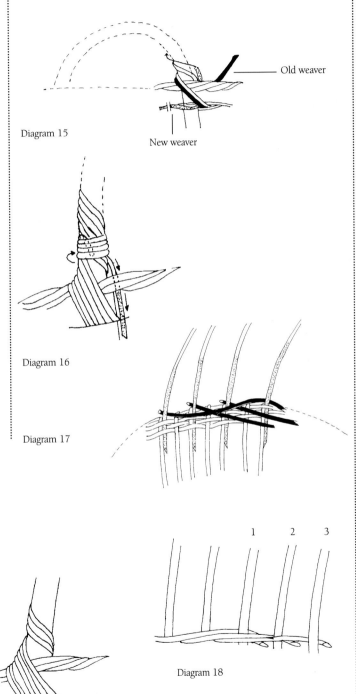

Diagram 15 — Old weaver — New weaver

Diagram 16

Diagram 17

Diagram 18

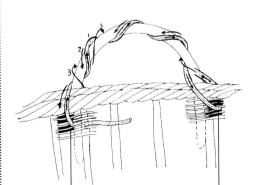

Start close to handle & wrap to left

Start as far right as you can & wrap in towards handle on left

Diagram 13

First wrap

Diagram 14

Gardening Tool Basket

This basket was designed by Dianne Craver of Candler, North Carolina. It is sturdy and useful for carrying garden tools or even basketmaking tools. The divider helps keep everything organized.

APPROXIMATE SIZE

11" x 14" x 10" high

MATERIALS

14" wide x 10" high D handle
3/4" flat reed (stakes)
1/2" flat reed (weavers and base fillers)
3/8" flat reed (divider)
1/2" flat oval reed (rim)
#2 or #3 seagrass (rim filler)
3/16" flat reed (lashing)

PRELIMINARY STEP

From the 3/4" flat reed, cut:
- 11 pieces 24" long
- 8 pieces 29" long
- 11 pieces 18" long

From the 1/2" flat reed, cut:
- 6 pieces 20" long
- 8 pieces 24" long

From the 3/8" flat reed, cut 1 piece 20" long.

MAKING THE BASE

Mark all the centers of all the pieces on the wrong (rough) side. Also, mark the center of the bottom of the handle.

Soak the pieces for several minutes until pliable.

Lay 6 of the 24" pieces of 3/4" flat reed horizontally, wrong side up, aligning the center marks. Space them evenly so the measurement from side to side is 11".

Lay the handle vertically on top of the 6 stakes. See **Diagram 1**.

Lay the other five 24" pieces horizontally on top of the handle.

Using both the eight 24" pieces of 1/2" flat and the eight 29" pieces of 3/4" flat, weave the base alternating overs and unders. Begin by weaving a piece of 1/2" on each side of the handle and alternate sizes (1/2" and 3/4") ending with a piece of 3/4" on both sides. See **Diagram 1**. *Note:* The first row on each side of the handle is woven in the same pattern as the handle. Pack the base pieces closely together so there are no "holes." Measure and true the base to 11" x 14".

MAKING THE DIVIDER

Upsett the stakes by bending them over upon themselves toward the center of the base. See **Diagram 2**.

On the 20" piece of 3/8" flat reed (the divider bar), make a center mark. Lay the 3/8" piece on the base with the center mark aligned with the center mark on the handle.

Make marks on the 3/8" piece to correspond with the stakes that are woven perpendicular to the handle. See **Diagram 3**.

Soak the 11 pieces of 3/4" flat that were cut 18" long (the divider stakes), then fold them in half, wrong sides together. Lay them over the 3/8" piece (bar) on the marked spaces. See **Diagram 4**. Hold the stakes on the bar

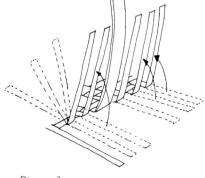

Diagram 1

Diagram 2

with clothespins.

Using the 6 pieces of 1/2" flat (20" long), weave over and under the divider stakes, aligning the center marks with the center stake. See **Diagram 5**. Leave the ends extended freely...sides and ends.

Push the ends of the stakes under the woven stakes in the base of the basket. Bend the ends of the divider weavers alternately right and left. See **Diagram 6**. They will be woven in as the sides are woven.

Bend the stakes sharply at the base of the divider so they will lie flat in the base. Adjust the divider stakes, if necessary, to match the position of those in the basket.

FINISHING THE BASKET

Soak several long pieces of 1/2" flat reed. Begin weaving around the basket, as in **Diagram 7**, in a plain over-under weave. End a row as in **Diagram 8**, overlapping 4 stakes and cutting the weaver so it is hidden behind a stake. Make sure the weavers are woven right side out. Do not weave the 1/2" filler pieces. Leave them

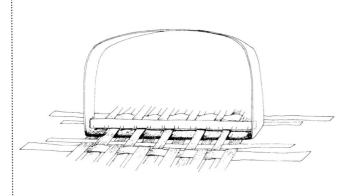

Diagram 3

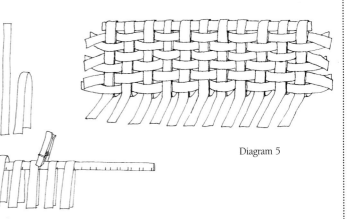

Diagram 4

Diagram 5

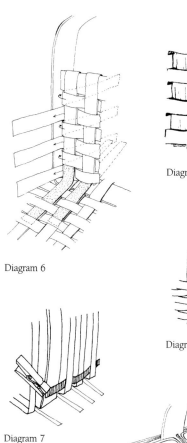

Diagram 6

Diagram 7

Diagram 8

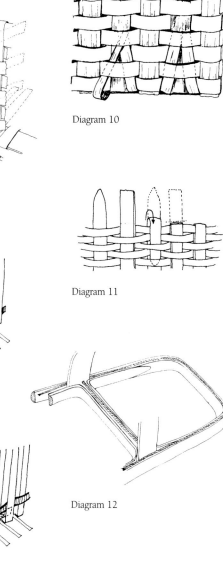

Diagram 10

Diagram 11

Diagram 12

lying flat until 5 or 6 rows are woven.

Weave the ends of the divider weavers in as you are weaving the rows. See **Diagram 9**. Weave 6 start-stop rows.

If necessary, rewet the filler strips, bend them up and tuck them under several rows of weaving. See **Diagram 10**.

Cut all the stakes on the inside of the top row of weaving flush with the top row.

Point all the stakes on the outside of the basket, rewet them if necessary, bend them over to the inside of the basket and tuck them behind the first available row of weaving. See **Diagram 11**.

Soak 2 pieces of 1/2" flat oval. One of them should be long enough to reach around the outside of the basket. The other piece should reach around half the inside and the one side of the divider. Also soak a very long piece of 3/16" flat reed for lashing and seagrass to fill the rim around the basket and the divider.

Place the soaked 1/2" flat oval around the top row of weaving on the outside of the basket, allowing the ends to overlap 2" to 3". Mark the

overlap and remove to shave the ends where they overlap. Bevel the overlapped area so it is no thicker than a single thickness of 1/2" flat oval. Replace it when the ends are beveled and hold it in place with clothespins.

Place another soaked piece of 1/2" flat oval around the inside rim of the basket, going around the inside wall of half the inside and one side of the divider wall. Repeat on the other side of the basket inside (and the other side of the divider). Mark the overlap. Remove and plane the ends as before. Replace and hold all pieces in place with clothespins. See **Diagram 12 & 12A**.

Begin lashing on the divider wall at one end. Hook the end of the weaver over the wall, under the 2 rim pieces and lash in place as in **Diagram 13**, going over all the rim pieces and through each space between stakes. When the divider is lashed in place, continue lashing around the basket, ending where you began on the basket rim. End lashing, as you began, by hiding the ends between the rim pieces or inside the basket behind a weaver.

Diagram 9

Diagram 12A

outside rim

inside rim

Diagram 13

SOUTHWESTERN

This basket is compliments of Genie Jackson, a very talented basketmaker and designer who lives in Coral Springs, Florida. It teaches several round reed techniques and produces a lovely urn-shaped basket that could be used to hold flowers or perhaps even some rolled towels.

APPROXIMATE SIZE
9" diameter X 9" high

MATERIALS NEEDED
#3 round reed (weavers; approx. 1/2 lb.)
#2 round reed (weavers; 8 pcs. approx. 6' long)
#4 round reed (weavers; 4 pcs. approx 36" long)
#3 round reed, dyed (weavers, dyed for color band)
#5 round reed (spokes)

Southwest Urn

PRELIMINARY STEP
Using #3 round reed, dye 4 long pieces in each of the following colors: peach, sky blue, lavender, rose.

WEAVING THE BASE
From the #5 round reed, cut 8 pieces 7" long. Mark the center of each piece. Also from the #5 round reed, cut 28 pieces 22" long. Soak the 7" spokes and the #2 round pieces until they are pliable. Split 4 of the 7" spokes through the center with an awl for about 1" (1/2" on each side of the center mark). See **Diagram 1**. Insert the other four 7" spokes through all the split ones and center them so there are 4 spokes each way forming a cross. See **Diagram 2**.

Pinch and fold a long "piece" of #2 round reed about 2 feet from one end. Mentally (or physically) letter the groups of spokes A through D as in **Diagram 3**.

Loop the fold around group A as in **Diagram 3** with the short weaver (1) behind A. To "reverse twine," weaver #1 moves over the next group of spokes crossing over weaver #2. Weaver 2 falls into place behind the next group (B). Continue this movement, turning the base in a counterclockwise direction while weaving in a clockwise direction, each time bringing the "behind" weaver over the next group (**Diagrams 4 & 5**). One complete revolution is shown in **Diagram 6**.

Continue these movements, turning the cross after every stroke so the spokes being covered are always on the right. This section of the base is completed when there are 4 rows of weaving showing on all groups of spokes. End the short weaver in the angle between A and B.

With the long weaver, continue to weave, separating the spokes in Japanese weave, over 2 spokes and behind 1 with the single weaver (see **Diagram 7**). Separate the spokes evenly and keep the rounds close together. To add a new weaver, allow the old weaver to end under a spoke and tuck in to the left of that spoke. Tuck the new weaver to the right of the previous spoke, and carry it over the tuck of the old weaver and behind the next spoke and

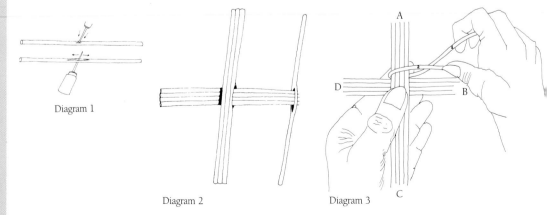

Diagram 1

Diagram 2

Diagram 3

continue with the Japanese weave. See **Diagram 8**.

The base should be slightly domed. To create that effect, push up on the base with the palm of your hand or hold the edge of the base in the palm and push up with your fingers. See **Diagram 9**.

Continue to Japanese weave until the base measures 5" across. End the weaver by tucking it beside a spoke.

BI-SPOKING & UPSETTING THE SIDES

Soak the 22" long "side" spokes and point them on one side of one end.

Insert the pointed end of the spokes, one on each side of 3 consecutive spokes for about 1" into the weaving. Insert only 1 new spoke to the left of every fourth spoke. At the same time you are inserting new spokes, trim the base spokes as near to the Japanese weave as possible. The "domed" side

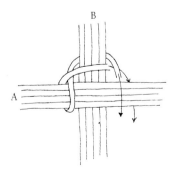

Diagram 4

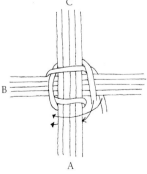

Diagram 5

Diagram 6

Diagram 7

New weaver

Old weaver

Diagram 8

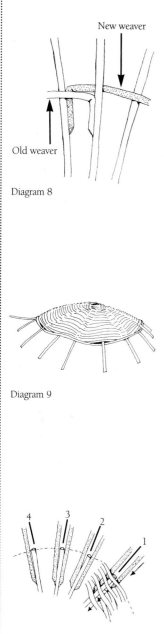

Diagram 9

Diagram 10

3-ROD WALE

Triple weave, or 3-rod wale, for 1 round by bringing the farthest left weaver in front of 2 spokes and behind the third and out. Continue to do this, always picking up the left weaver until the weaver comes out to the left of the marked spoke. See

or the side covered by over twos is the inside of the basket. An awl will help to open up the space into which the spoke is inserted. See **Diagram 10**.

To separate the side spokes equidistantly, 1 row of 3-rod arrow is needed. Three-rod arrow consists of 1 row of triple weave (3-rod wale), a step up, and 1 row of reverse triple weave. Cut 3 pieces of #3 round reed, each measuring at least twice the circumference of the base, and place one end behind 3 consecutive spokes. Mark the first spoke of the 3, as it is the first spoke of the arrow.

Diagram 11.

STEP-UP

Now using the weaver on the right, weave in front of 2 spokes, to the right, behind 1 and out, as in **Diagram 12**. Take the next (middle) weaver to the right in front of 2 spokes, behind 1 and out. Take the remaining weaver to the right in front of 2 spokes, behind 1 and out. The step-up is complete. See **Diagram 13**.

REVERSE 3-ROD WALE

To form the second half of the arrow, start the triple weave again with the weaver on the left. Weave in front of 2 spokes, but make the weaver go under the other 2 weavers, behind 1 spoke and out. See **Diagram 14**.

Continue in this manner, always using the left weaver until the weaver comes out on the left of the marked spoke.

To end the 3-rod arrow, the first (left) weaver passes

in front of 2 spokes, goes under the top 2 weavers and ends behind spoke 1, to be cut later. See **Diagram 15**.

The second weaver moves in front of 2 spokes, under the remaining weaver to the right and also under the top weaver in place, ending behind spoke 2.

The third weaver passes in front of 2 spokes and the 2 weavers which are the first and second stroke of the second row of the arrow and ends behind spoke 3. Cut the ends short and at an angle, making them conform to the shape of the base when the basket is dry.

Before upsetting the sides, soak the basket base, side spokes and some #4 round reed well. With needle nose pliers, pinch the side spokes close to the weaving of the arrow. A 4-rod coil is used to upsett the base. With side spokes pointing upward, insert 4 weavers of #4 round reed behind 4 consecutive

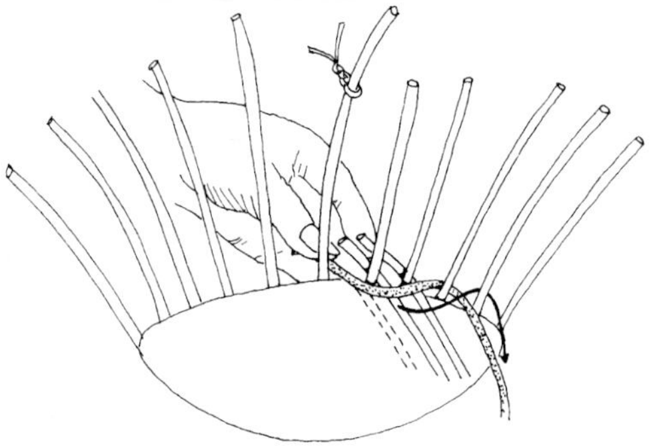

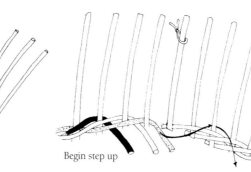

Diagram 11

Begin step up

Diagram 12

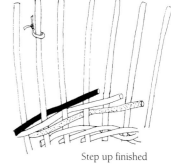

Step up finished

Diagram 13

72

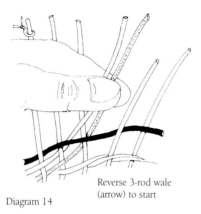

Reverse 3-rod wale
(arrow) to start

Diagram 14

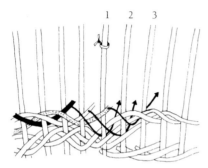

Ending 3-rod arrow 1st step

Diagram 15

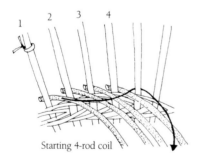

Starting 4-rod coil

Diagram 16

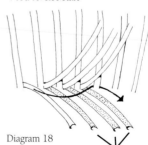

Locking the 4-rod coil

Diagram 17

spokes. Mark the #1 spoke. Remember you are now working on the outside of the basket and hold the base with the underside toward you. To do a 4-rod coil, you will take each farthest "left" weaver in front of 3 spokes, behind 1 spoke and out to the front. See **Diagram 16**. Guide the direction of the spokes as you weave so they turn evenly and are the same distance apart. Weave 1 row of the 4-rod coil, always moving the weaver on the left. End weavers behind spokes where they started. Lock the coil by lifting in order from right to left the ends of the weavers, D, C, B and A, and slip the final ends between them and the spoke. The final end of D goes under the beginning of D. Cut the ends at an angle when dry, close to the weaving. See **Diagram 17**.

WEAVING THE SIDES
Triple weave the sides with natural #3 round reed for about 5- 1/2 ". Allow the sides to flare a little. By the time 5" of weaving is done, the diameter of the basket should be about 9". End weavers behind spokes where they started, and cut at an angle when dry.

Using the 4 different colors of #3 round, weave 3 rows of 4-rod arrow, each row of which consists of: (1) One row of 4-rod wale (explained previously in **Diagram 16**); (2) a step-up, which is the same as a 3-rod wale step-up (just done with 4 weavers instead of 3), as in **Diagrams 12 & 13**; and (3) a row of 4-rod reverse wale. Four-rod reverse wale is done exactly like 4-rod wale, except that the farthest left weaver must move under the 3 weavers to the right of it, behind the fourth spoke and out to the front. See **Diagram 18**. (4) Work a lock-in to end the first arrow; the first weaver passes in front of and under the other 3 weavers and ends behind the

4-rod reverse start

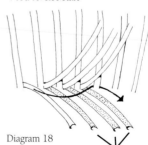

Diagram 18

These 3 are lifted up for first weaver on left to pass under starting spoke. See **Diagram 19**. The second weaver passes in front and under the other 2 weavers and also under the weaving already in place, ending behind spoke 2. The third and fourth weavers end in the same manner.

Do not cut off any weavers, as you will continue to make 2 more sets of arrows. Start your next row of a 4-rod coil by bringing your weaver back to the outside of basket behind the original starting 4 spokes. Complete 2 more sets of 4-rod arrows. At the end of the final set the weavers will be cut off short. Avoid adding new weavers during this step-up at the start of each new row, as it could easily cause mistakes. Rewet the tops of the spokes and triple weave (3-rod wale) with #3 natural round reed for 8 rows, or about 1-1/2". As you weave this section, push inward on the spokes and pull gently on the weavers to obtain the urn shape. End weavers behind the same spokes as they started and cut them at an angle when dry.

MAKING THE BORDER

Soak spokes thoroughly before weaving the border. With needle nose pliers, pinch the spokes just above the last row of weaving. Take any spoke behind the 2 spokes to the right and to the outside. See **Diagram 20**.

When you have returned to the starting point, 2 spokes will remain. Pull up the beginning spoke a little and push the far left remaining spoke under it. Then pull up the second woven spoke so the last spoke can be pushed through. See **Diagram 21**.

Next move each spoke over 2 spokes to the right and insert it to the inside of the basket, going under the loop formed by the first row of the border. See **Diagram 22**.

The last 2 rows are worked on the inside of the basket. Hold 3 spokes out, bring the left spoke over the right 2, and drop it down next to the side of the basket. See **Diagram 23**.

Each row is ended when you have 2 spokes remaining. To find where to tuck the far left spoke, push up on the beginning spoke. Again bring the far left spoke to the right and tuck into the loop formed by pushing up the beginning spoke. Now push up the second spoke and tuck the remaining spoke into the loop formed nearest the basket edge. See **Diagram 24**.

Repeat this row, taking each spoke over 2 spokes to the right and ending just as before. Be sure to keep spokes wet while working the border. Cut spokes to approximately 1/2" when border is complete.

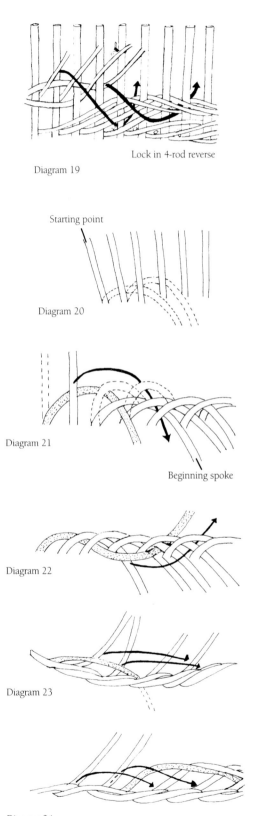

Lock in 4-rod reverse

Diagram 19

Starting point

Diagram 20

Diagram 21

Beginning spoke

Diagram 22

Diagram 23

Diagram 24

Swirling Star Bowl

Many thanks to Joan Moore of Highland, Michigan, for sharing this lovely bowl with us. Make it to match your color scheme and Southwestern decor. Shown also is the "optional start." Make either or, better yet, make both.

APPROXIMATE SIZE

15" diameter x 4" deep

MATERIALS NEEDED

1/4" or 7mm flat oval or heavy 1/4" flat reed (spokes)
1/4" or 7mm flat oval, light weight (weavers)
3/16" flat reed (rim)
1/2" or 3/8" flat oval reed (rim)
Fine cane (lashing)
#5 or #6 round reed (rim filler)

PRELIMINARY STEP

Cut 38 spokes 26" long. Dye 16 a light color, 16 a dark color and 6 a medium color, or use any 3 colors of your choice. Mark the centers on the rough or flat side. Soak all the pieces before beginning to weave the base.

WEAVING THE BASE

The base is woven with the *wrong* (flat) side up. The first 16 spokes are the lightest color. Beginning at the center of the base with a light spoke, place 1 vertically. Lay the second piece of light perpendicular to the first, aligning center marks. See **Diagram 1**.

Note: **Diagram 1A** shows an optional start with 1 dark vertical piece and 1 dark horizontal piece. Then return to the regular pattern.

Lay the third, fourth, fifth and sixth pieces as in **Diagram 2**. Spokes 1 and 2 are center spokes. Align center marks on other spokes with the 2 center spokes. Continuing to use the light color, lay the seventh, eight, ninth and tenth pieces as in **Diagram 3**. Lay the eleventh, twelfth, thirteenth and fourteenth pieces as in **Diagram 4**.

As in **Diagram 5**, lay the last 2 light pieces (fifteenth and sixteenth) vertically, one on each side of the center. Until now, pieces have simply been laid on top of others. From now on, newly added spokes will be woven under and over existing spokes.

Changing to the dark spokes, the seventeenth and eighteenth spokes are woven under spoke 1 and over the others. See **Diagram 5**. As shown in **Diagram 6**, dark spoke 19 is woven under the center spoke, as is spoke 20. Dark spokes 21 and 22 are woven under the center 3 spokes and over the others.

As **Diagram 7** indicates, spokes 23 to 32 are dark and are woven in the following pattern:

Row 23: under center 3, over the others
Row 24: under center 3, over the others
Row 25: under center 5, over the others
Row 26: under center 5, over the others
Row 27: under center 5, over the others
Row 28: under center 5, over the others
Row 29: under center 7, over the others
Row 30: under center 7, over the others
Row 31: under center 7, over the others
Row 32: under center 7, over the others
Rows 33 to 38 are woven

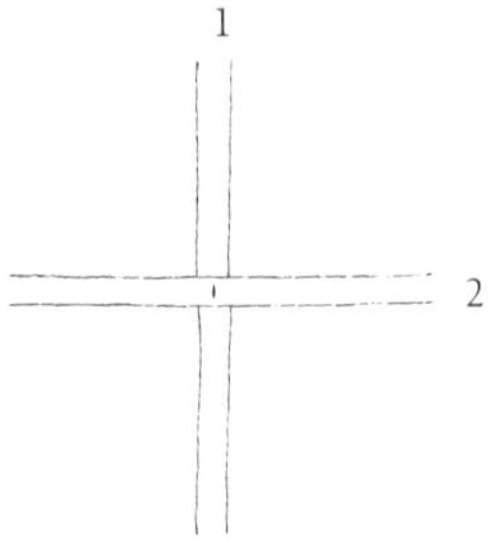

Diagram 1

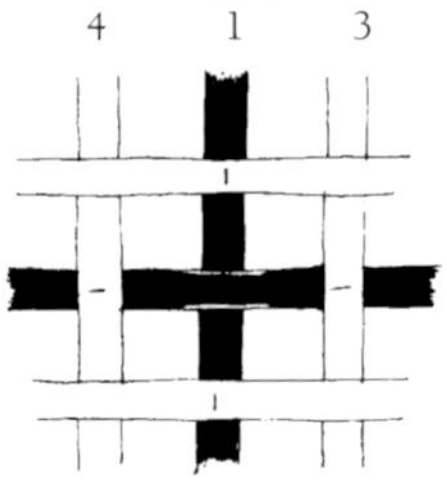

Diagram 1A

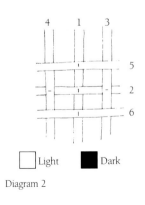

Diagram 2

with the medium color in the following pattern:

Row 33: over center 1; under 4 on each side, over others

Row 34: over center 1; under 4 on each side, over others

Row 35: over center 1; under 4 on each side, over others

Row 36: over center 1; under 4 on each side, over others

Row 37: over center 3; under 4 on each side, over others

Row 38: over center 3; under 4 on each side, over others

Tighten the spokes so there is no space between them. The base should measure approximately 4-1/2" x 5".

WEAVING THE SIDES

Turn the base over with the flat oval side of the reed up now.

Soak a long flexible piece of natural 1/4" flat oval reed for several minutes until it is very pliable. Cut it in half lengthwise, making it 1/8". As in **Diagram 8**, taper the end of one of the split pieces for 1" to 2" and begin weaving on one side by going over 3, under 2, etc. If you

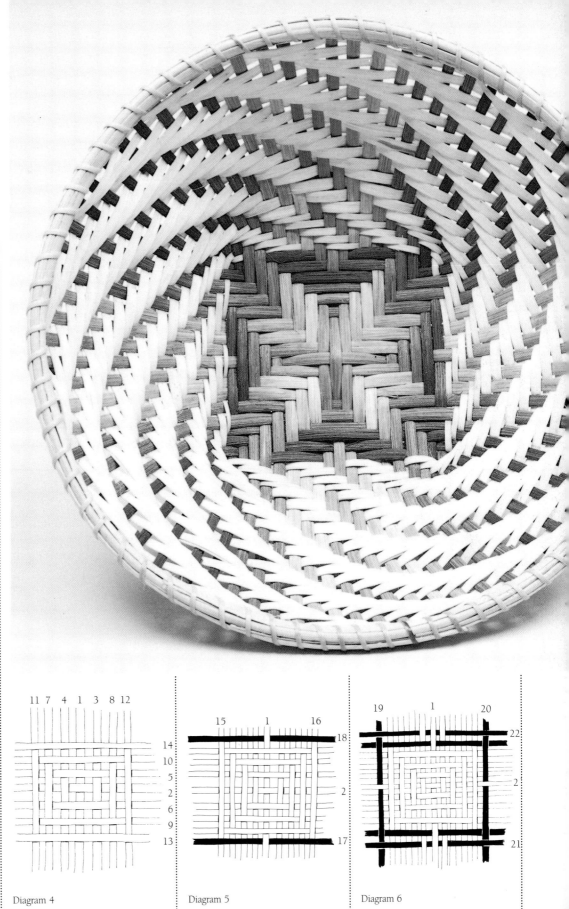

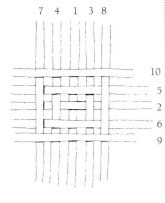

Diagram 3

Diagram 4

Diagram 5

Diagram 6

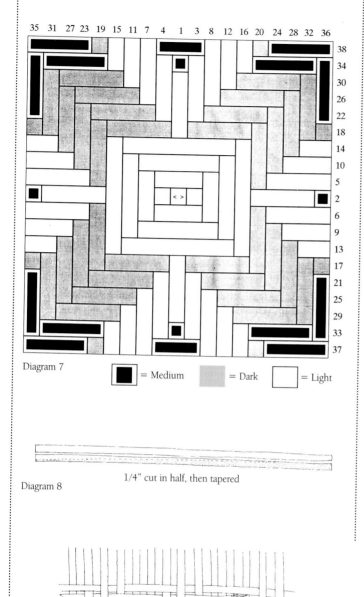

35 31 27 23 19 15 11 7 4 1 3 8 12 16 20 24 28 32 36

| | 38 |
| 34 |
| 30 |
| 26 |
| 22 |
| 18 |
| 14 |
| 10 |
| 5 |
| 2 |
| 6 |
| 9 |
| 13 |
| 17 |
| 21 |
| 25 |
| 29 |
| 33 |
| 37 |

Diagram 7

■ = Medium   ▨ = Dark   □ = Light

Diagram 8

1/4" cut in half, then tapered

Diagram 9

tail

Diagram 11

Splicing new weaver

Diagram 10

are right-handed, weave to the left for now, so when you hold the basket you will be working from the outside weaving from left to right. (If you are left-handed, weave to the right for the moment.)

Note: Leave a tail sticking out when you begin. As the weaver goes around once and returns to the starting point, go over the tail to secure it when you begin the second round. Weave over 3, under 2 in a continuous weave (when the end of a row is reached, continue around the basket again; the over 3 "steps over" 1 spoke automatically). See **Diagram 9**.

Note: In order for the "swirl" pattern to be most effective, you must keep the spokes relatively close together—no farther apart than 1/4".

Weave the first 3 rows around with the base flat on a table. Do not attempt to make the sides stand yet. As you weave the first several rows, make the spokes move toward their respective corners, thus creating a "sunburst" with the corners filled with spokes. See **Diagram 10**.

After 3 rows of weaving around the base and forcing the spokes to move and fill in the corners, the sides may start to stand a little on their own. You may lift the base and hold it with spokes pointed away from you and weave from the outside of the basket. If you find the sides going up too fast, put the basket back on the table and weave from the inside. Just the presence of your hands inside the basket will make the sides lean out. See **Diagram 11** for how to add on a new weaver when one runs out. If necessary, shave some of the oval side from overlapped area.

Continue weaving around the basket until there are approximately 2-1/2" of the spokes remaining. Taper the end again to 1/8" wide and end the weaving directly above the starting spot. See **Diagram 12**.

Weave 2 rows of start-stop weaving with 3/16" flat or flat oval reed. Begin a soaked weaver on top of a spoke, weave around the basket going over 1 spoke, under the next, etc. End the row by going over the beginning to the fourth spoke. Cut the weaver behind the fourth spoke. See **Diagram 13**. Start and stop the next row in a different place.

Point the spokes on the *inside* of the basket, rewet them if they are dry, bend them over the top row of weaving and tuck them into the weaving on the *outside* of the basket. Cut the spokes that are on the outside of the basket flush with the top row of weaving. See **Diagram 14**.

APPLYING THE RIM

Measure around the top of the basket and add 3" or 4" for overlapping. Cut the pieces of 1/2" flat oval

according to the measurements. Mark off the areas of overlap and, with a knife or plane, shave both ends (top of one and bottom of the other) so their thickness is no greater than that of a single thickness of 1/2" flat oval. See **Diagram 15**.

Place the 1/2" flat oval around the top of the basket, covering the top 2 rows of 3/16" flat reed with the overlapped areas near, but not on top of, each other. Lay a piece of #6 round reed between the 2 rim pieces with ends beveled for several inches like the rim. See **Diagram 16**. Begin lashing just past the 2 areas of overlap by hiding the end of the lasher under the rim. Hook the end over the basket wall as in **Diagram 17**. Bring the lasher around the rim pieces and through each space under the rim between spokes. End the lasher as it began or discreetly secure the end behind a weaver on the outside of the basket.

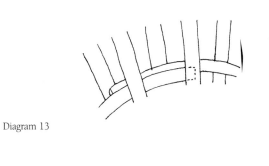

Diagram 13

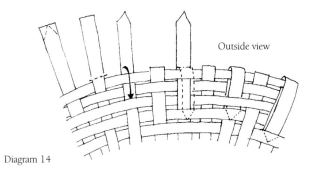

Outside view

Diagram 14

Diagram 15

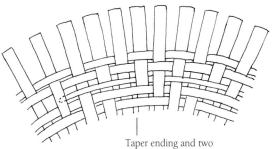

Diagram 16

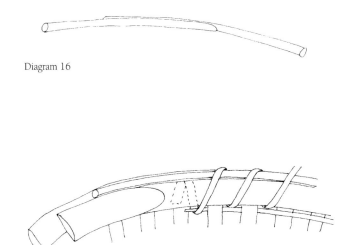

Diagram 12

Taper ending and two rows of start + stop

Diagram 17

Hopi Wicker Tray

This wonderful Hopi tray was made by Dianne Stanton of Pembroke, Massachusetts. She gives credit to Carol Hart, who taught her the technique. It is made from round reed instead of the traditional rabbit brush, sumac shoots and yucca. It is a wonderful addition to a basket collection or to a Southwest style room.

APPROXIMATE SIZE
11" diameter

MATERIALS
#3 round reed (spokes)
#1 or #0 round reed
  (weavers)
3 colors of dye

This basket has been made for many years by the Hopi Indians. The traditional warp elements are sumac shoots, willow or wild currant; the weft is rabbit brush, and the rim wrapping is yucca painted with red ochre. The white coloration that is often seen results from bleaching the stems and whitewashing them with clay.

Since so few of us will ever have access to any of these wonderful natural materials, we must try to make clever copies. Dye approximately 1/3 hank of #0 or #1 round reed in 3 different colors. The colors used here were rust, gold and green, but that is entirely your choice.

STARTING THE BASE

Throughout the weaving of this basket, the warp groups will remain filled with enough warp pieces to keep the tension tight so the weavers can be packed down next to each other. That way, very little warp shows through the weaving. Also, all ends will be tucked in so both surfaces are clean.

The basket is started by weaving 2 centers. Each center consists of 8 spokes, arranged in pairs. From #3 round reed, cut 16 pieces about 20" long. Soak them for a few minutes, then mark the centers and 1" on each side of the centers on all the pieces. Also soak 2 long pieces of the gold weavers.

Note: Even though the colors are your choice and you may use any color any-where you want, specific colors will be given for particular areas.

As in **Diagram 1**, begin weaving over and under the 4 pairs of spokes, leaving a tail that can later be pushed down into the weaving. Start weaving on the 1" mark and weave to the other 1" mark, all the while holding the spokes so the distance across is 2". This, of course, will produce a 2" square. Repeat the procedure on the other 8 spokes (in pairs) with the same color weaver. When the 2 centers are finished, the weavers should be in the positions of the weavers in **Diagram 2**—1 at the bottom left and 1 at the bottom right. Next, as in **Diagram 3**, turn group B end over end, so its weaver is now at the top right. Then rotate B 90 degrees and lay it on top of A so the weavers are on the same side (left) with the weaver from B at the top. See **Diagram 4**. It will be the lead weaver and you will chase weave the

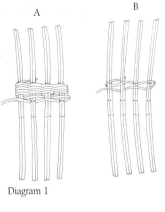

Diagram 1

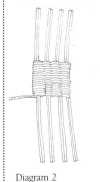

Diagram 2

Flip B over end to end

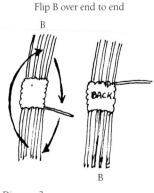

Diagram 3

entire basket. **Diagram 5** shows the weaver from B starting to weave with the arrows showing its future path until it catches up with the weaver from A. The weaver closest to the center is the one you should always use. **Diagram 6** shows 1 row made with B and then a chasing row made with A. To add a new weaver, as in **Diagram 7**, push the old end into the weaving beside a spoke immediately after the over stroke, and add the new one by pushing the end into the weaving beside the spoke before.

ADDING SPOKES

This basket is weft-faced, which means that the weaving (weft) will cover most of the spokes so that more of the pattern shows. After every 2 rounds of weaving, much packing is needed. A bent-tip awl or the nose of needle nose pliers will help in pushing the rows together toward the center. As the diameter of the basket gets

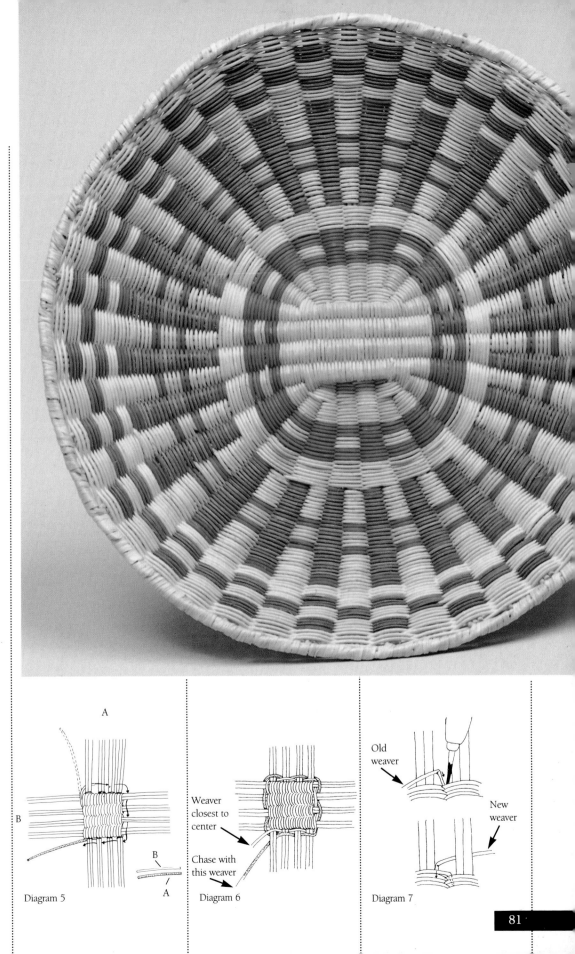

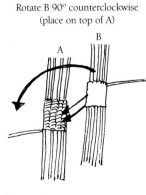

Rotate B 90° counterclockwise
(place on top of A)

A
B

Diagram 4

A

B

B
A

Diagram 5

Weaver closest to center

Chase with this weaver

Diagram 6

Old weaver

New weaver

Diagram 7

larger, the spaces between the groups will increase and the weavers will not pack down as tightly. When this happens, you need to add spokes to each group to increase the friction.

Cut 8 new spokes that extend as far as the original ones after being inserted. Slype the ends (cut 1 side at an angle) and insert them into the corners, between the 2 corner spokes. See **Diagram 8**. Each corner pair gets a single new spoke between them. Begin weaving again with the weaver closest to the center. As in **Diagram 9**, weave over the first 2 spokes of the newly formed group of 3. Then weave over the remaining 1 as a single. In the next group of 3, weave over the first 1 as a single and then the next 2 as a pair. Continue around the base in like manner with 1 weaver and then the other in alternate overs and unders as always. Weave and chase 2 more times around before

adding more stakes. **Diagram 10** shows several rows of weaving after the addition of the first 8 new spokes. Always cut new spokes so they are extended as far as the original ones. **Diagram 11** shows new single spokes being added to the singles that remained from the other addition. Weave several more rows until the weavers begin to slip; then, as in **Diagram 12**, add a third spoke between the pairs. **Diagram 13** illustrates the fourth spoke being added to the left of the 3. In **Diagram 14** the 4 have been split, creating pairs again. **Diagram 15** shows new spokes being added, after many rows of weaving, between the pairs to create 3s again. The diameter of your basket will determine how many times you need to add spokes. Just remember to add spokes anytime the weaving starts to slip, or when you can't pack the weaving down any more.

SHAPING OF THE TRAY

The traditional basket is either bowl-shaped or a flat plaque with a slightly raised "hump," or center. If you want a plaque, you need to think about keeping the center up and forcing the spokes away from you so the center will be higher. If you are making a bowl, the center can be flat. Eventually, you will make the sides rise by pushing on the spokes and pulling on the weavers to make the spaces between the spokes smaller.

FORMING THE PATTERN

The patterns for Hopi plaques are based on using many different colors and changing them at specific intervals. This simple one uses 3 geometric and circular patterns. The first one was woven after the corners were formed and before the groups of 4 were divided into sets of 2 with the gold color.

End the gold weavers and change to rust. Weave 3

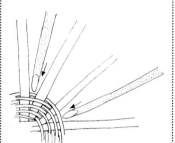

Diagram 8

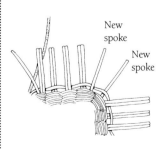

Diagram 9

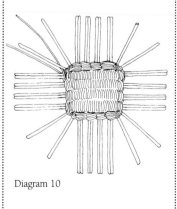

Diagram 10

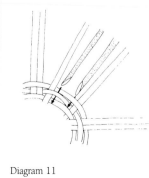

Diagram 11

Diagram 12

New spoke

New spoke

rounds with both weavers the same color (rust), then change one of the weavers to natural and weave with the 2 different colors for 3 rounds. End the natural one and replace it with rust so they are both the same again. In **Diagrams 13** and **14**, you can see a "spot" of a different color, which means that one weaver was changed to a different color.

The second pattern starts after the groups of 4 are broken into sets of 2. It looks like vertical bands connected by a circular ring. The pattern begins with 2 weavers the same color (natural, in this case) to create a background. Weave 5 or 6 rows of background in natural. Then change one of the weavers to rust for 3 rows. This weaver will create the vertical band and will keep changing colors while the other one will remain natural until it too changes, which will create the round band. After the 3 rows of rust,

change the same weaver to green for 5 or 6 rows. End and change the natural weaver to rust for 2 rows, then gold for 3 rows, then back to rust again, all the while keeping the other weaver green. After a few rows, you will realize that you can easily create your own designs just by changing the colors of weavers. It is, however, important to start and stop the weavers at the same place every row so the bands will be even. The third geometric pattern on the basket shown is a checkerboard. To weave it, first weave 3 rows of background (both weavers in natural), then change 1 weaver to green. Weave 3 rows and swap colors of weavers. Weave 3 rows and swap back to the original. Continue swapping colors for as many rows as you want. Finish with 3 or 4 rows of background.

MAKING THE BORDER
This is a compound type

border. It resembles coiling and is very easy to execute. The remaining spokes should be soaked until pliable and pinched with needle nose pliers so they will bend sideways. Cut 2 of the spokes flush with the last row of weaving so that the remaining spoke will reach the fourth spoke beyond itself. Bend down 3 spokes and hold them together so they all touch each other. See **Diagram 16**. With the wider end of a soaked and flattened piece of raffia, start wrapping over the bent spokes as in **Diagram 16**. Keep bending the spokes over and wrapping around them, adding on to the raffia as needed. See **Diagram 17**. Both the butt and tip ends of the raffia can get caught in the bundle as you wrap. At the end, thread the raffia on a tapestry needle and feed it through the space under the last 3 spokes. The last end of the raffia can be threaded into the bundle.

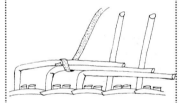

Diagram 16

Diagram 13

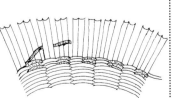

Diagram 14

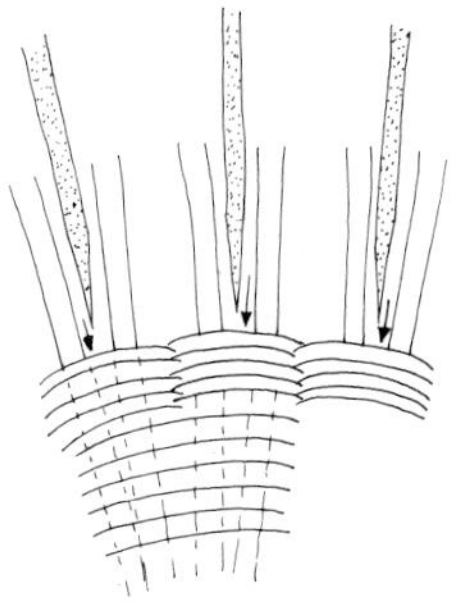

Diagram 15

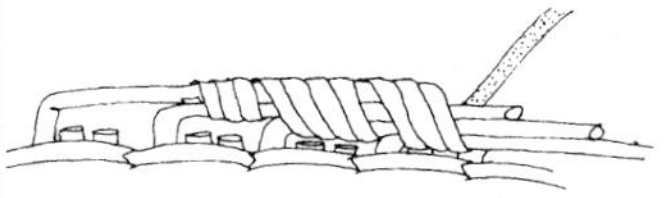

Diagram 17

Southwest Trinket Bowl

Patti Hawkins of Pace, Florida, originally used this pattern in the configuration of a rectangular tray. For us, she used the same pattern but made a round bowl. It is a twill pattern in three colors and is similar to the Hopi plaited ring basket. The challenge lies in continuing the base pattern on the sides so it is difficult to discern where the base ends and the sides begin. In the very narrow flat oval reed, it is wonderfully intricate and is quite striking on a wall, mantle or table.

APPROXIMATE SIZE

7-1/2" diameter x 2" high

MATERIALS NEEDED

11/64" (very supple) flat oval reed (spokes and weavers)
7mm or 1/4" flat oval reed (rim)
#4 round reed (rim filler)
Fine cane used wrong side up (lasher)
Peach, sky blue and mint green dye

PRELIMINARY STEP

From the 11/64" flat oval reed, cut 44 pieces 15" long for spokes.

Dye: 16 spokes blue
14 spokes peach
14 spokes green

Also dye 3 or 4 long pieces of 11/64 flat oval reed each of the colors. Dye a piece of rim material, lasher and #4 round reed all green.

WEAVING THE BASE

o = over   u = under

The layout of the base, horizontally and vertically, is primarily an over 3, under 3 twill except for the center section of 5 spokes. In these sections, the spokes will go over and under each other in a pattern of o5, o5, o3, u5, u5, u3.

Of the *horizontal* spokes, all of the green and blue spokes will follow the same weaving path next to each other. Of the *vertical* spokes, all the green and peach ones will be woven identically.

Note: Although the diagrams may show some space between spokes, in reality they should be "flush" together.

Soak the spokes briefly and wipe with a towel to avoid any bleeding of color. Mark the centers of all the pieces on the right (oval) side.

The base will be laid out with the oval side of the reed *up*.

As in **Diagram 1**, lay 5 spokes horizontally in the following order: peach, blue, green, blue, peach.

Also in **Diagram 1**, lay a green spoke vertically over all 5 horizontal spokes, aligning center marks. Then lay a peach spoke on each side of the green one. Add a blue spoke to the outside of each peach spoke, going over spokes 2, 3 and 4, and under 1 and 5. There are now 5 vertical and 5 horizontal spokes.

You will now add 9 more vertical spokes on each side of the original section. Refer to **Diagram 2** as you weave. *Note:* **Diagram 2** shows the center 5 horizontal and vertical spokes unshaded for clarity only.

Adding vertical spokes to the right of the center 5, the first one will be a green piece that goes under all 5 horizontal spokes. The next one is peach and goes under all 5. Then a blue is placed under the center 3 and over the other 2. All the remaining vertical spokes will be added following the pattern u5, u5, u3, o5, o5, o3, u5, u5, u3 in the order of green, peach and blue.

After adding all 23 vertical spokes, pack them closely together.

You now need to add the

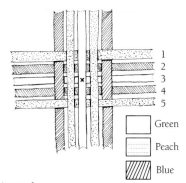

Green
Peach
Blue

Diagram 1

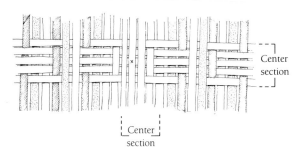

Center section

Center section

Diagram 2

remaining 8 horizontal spokes above the center section and 8 below as well. Regardless of whether they are above or below, they will be placed in the following order: green, blue, peach. *Each row is a 3/3 twill (o3, u3) pattern, except for the center sections, where the pattern is as follows:*

Row 1: Green spoke o5 center spokes

Row 2: Blue spoke o5 center spokes

Row 3: Peach spoke o3 center spokes

Row 4: Green spoke u5 center spokes

Row 5: Blue spoke u5 center spokes

Row 6: Peach spoke u3 center spokes

Row 7: Green spoke o5 center spokes

Row 8: Blue spoke o5 center spokes

Note: The rows may end up over or under fewer than 3 spokes because the row ran out. **Diagram 3** shows the weaving of the top half of

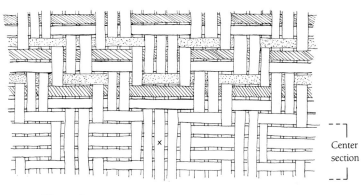

Center section

Diagram 3

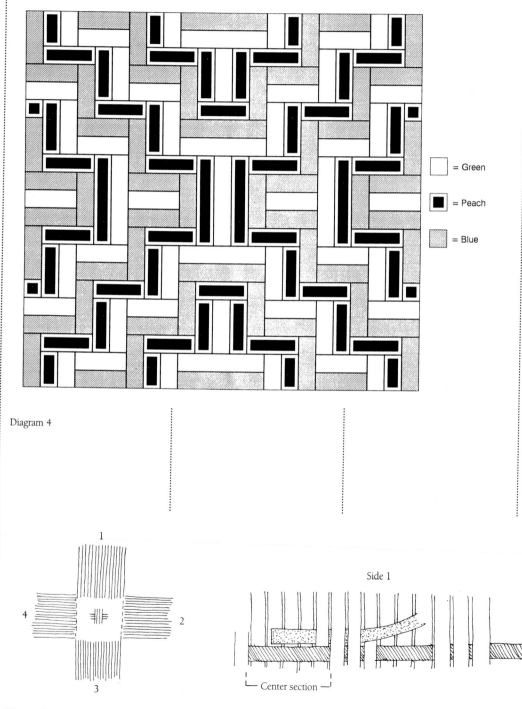

= Green

= Peach

= Blue

Diagram 4

the base. The center 5 horizontal and vertical spokes are unshaded for clarity only. The 8 rows below the center will be woven exactly like the ones above. The completed base will have 21 horizontal spokes and 23 vertical spokes and will measure approximately 3-3/4" x 4". See **Diagram 4** for the completed base.

WEAVING THE SIDES

Look at your base as you have laid it out with 21 horizontal spokes and 23 vertical spokes. To describe the side weaving, we will label the sides 1 to 4 as in **Diagram 5**.

As with the base, there are certain main points to understand for the sides: (1) this is primarily a 3/3 twill, except for some of the centers and corners; (2) on sides 1 and 3, each blue weaver will be woven identically to the green weaver just below it; (3) on sides 2 and 4, each green weaver is woven just like

Diagram 5

Diagram 6

Side 1

Center section

Last row of base

the peach weaver below it.

There are 13 rows of side weaving, alternating colors as you did in the base. Start weaving the first row on side 1, from left to right. See **Diagram 6**. All weaving is done in start-stop rows from the inside of the basket (smooth side of base and weavers facing you) so that you can achieve a shallow bowl shape. See **Diagram 7** for how to start and stop rows, overlapping the ends at least 6 spokes.

A detailed pattern for side rows is shown as follows:

Row 1: Peach, o3/u3 twill except for the centers of sides 2 and 4, where weaver goes under 5.

Row 2: Green, o3/u3 twill with the following exceptions: u5 center spokes on all sides and o5 around every corner.

Row 3: Blue, o3/u3 twill except u5 center spokes on sides 1 and 3.

Row 4: Peach, o3/u3 twill except o5 center spokes on sides 2 and 4. See **Diagram 8** for 4 rows of weaving on side 1.

See **Diagram 9** for a detailed illustration of a corner with 4 rows of weaving done.

Row 5: Green, o3/u3 twill except o5 each set of center spokes and u5 around each corner.

Row 6: Blue, o3/u3 twill except o5 center spokes on sides 1 and 3.

Row 7: Repeat row 1.

Row 8: Repeat row 2.

Row 9: Repeat row 3.

Row 10: Repeat row 4.

Row 11: Repeat row 5.

Row 12: Repeat row 6.

Row 13: Repeat row 1.

This description of the pattern on the side rows may appear confusing, if not overwhelming, at first. However, once you see your pattern emerging, it will become easier and you may not need to refer to the directions at all.

Weave the first 4 rows around the sides with the base flat on the table, keep-

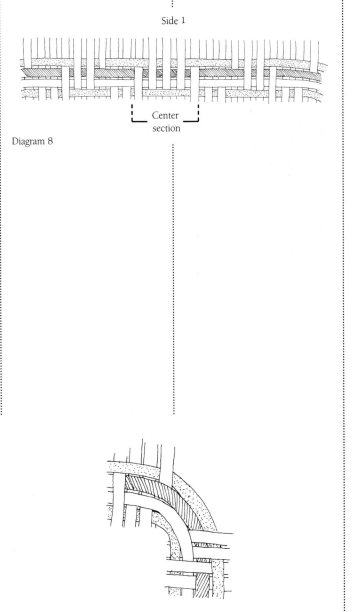

Side 1

Center section

Diagram 8

Diagram 9

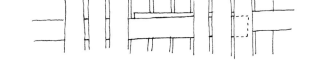

Diagram 7

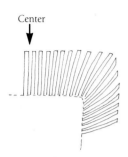

Center

Diagram 10

ing your tension snug around the corners and all weavers as close to each other as possible.

After completing these 4 rows, gently pull all spokes but the center ones toward the corners to create a sunburst effect. See **Diagram 10**. As you continue to weave, keep these spokes spread evenly apart and this will cause the basket to gradually pull up at the corners, creating a bowl shape. Do not pull the corners up too aggressively, or your bowl will not remain shallow. At the completion of 13 rows of weaving, your basket should only be about 1-1/2" to 2" high.

Pack all 13 rows of side weaving down well. Then weave 2 start-stop rows of over 1, under 1, using a dyed, soaked 11/64" weaver cut in half, lengthwise. These 2 rows, woven opposite each other, help "lock in" your weaving and keep the rows packed down as you prepare to apply the rim. See **Diagram 11**. **Diagram 12** shows ending these 2 rows.

The spokes that are on the outside of the last row of weaving will be cut flush with that top row of weaving. The ones that are on the inside of the last row of weaving are pointed and folded over the weaving and pushed down into the weaving on the outside of the basket. See **Diagram 13**.

APPLYING THE RIM

Soak a piece of 7mm flat oval reed (dyed green) that is long enough to reach around the top of the basket 2 times plus 5" or 6" for overlap. Place the flat oval around the inside and the outside of the basket, covering the top 2 rows of weaving. Allow the ends to overlap 2" or 3". The ends should be beveled with a knife or plane so the overlapped area is no thicker than a single thickness of the flat oval reed. Place the overlapped areas near, but not on top of, each other. Place a piece of #4 round reed (dyed green) between the 2 rim pieces, beveling the ends for 2" or 3" and overlapping them just as the rim pieces were overlapped.

Begin lashing with the dyed piece of fine cane, as in **Diagram 14**, just past the overlapped areas. Soak the lasher until it is pliable and begin lashing by hooking the end over the basket wall, taking it under the inside rim to begin. Lash all the pieces together by taking the lasher around all the rim pieces and through the spaces under the rim and between every 2 spokes.

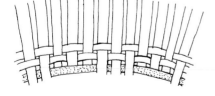

Diagram 11

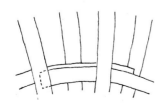

Diagram 12

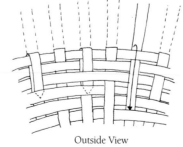

Outside View

Diagram 13

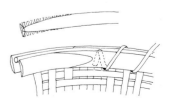

Diagram 14

Arrows Tray

This tray was designed and made by Eileen LaPorte of Romeo, Michigan. It is very sturdy and can be used as a functional serving tray or a purely decorative accessory piece in your home.

APPROXIMATE SIZE

12" diameter x 4-1/2" high

MATERIALS

1/2" flat reed (spokes)
1/4" or 7mm flat oval reed (spokes)
#3 round reed (twining)
3/8" flat reed (rim row)
1/2" flat oval reed (rim)
1/4" flat oval reed dyed 4 colors (arrows)
#6 round reed (rim filler)
Medium binder cane (lashing)
2 small bushel basket handles, 2-1/2" diameter

PREPARATION

Cut 48 pieces of 1/4" flat oval 18" long. Dye them in the following manner:
- 12 pieces light green or turquoise
- 12 pieces peach
- 12 pieces wine
- 12 pieces tan

WEAVING THE BASE

From the 1/2" flat reed, cut 12 pieces 30" long. Mark the centers of all the pieces on the wrong (rough) side. On 6 of the pieces mark 1-1/2" on either side of the center mark.

From the 1/4" flat oval reed, cut 24 pieces 20" long. Mark the centers of all these pieces on the wrong side and lay them aside for the moment.

Soak all the pieces for several minutes or until they are pliable. Lay the 6 pieces of 1/2" flat with the 1-1/2" marks like the spokes of a wheel, wrong side up. Lay pieces in the order shown in **Diagram 1**, with the first piece laid vertically and the second one perpendicular to it and alternating the rest of the pieces right and left.

Soak a long piece of #3 round reed for several minutes. Fold it about 12" off center. Place the fold around the first spoke and begin twining around all the spokes in a circle following the guide marks you made. See **Diagram 2**. Keep the spokes equidistant. Twine until there is enough space between all the spokes to add the other 6 spokes into the existing spaces. Lay these 6 spokes in the spaces as you come to them while twining around. See **Diagram 3**.

Add a new weaver as the old one runs out as in **Diagram 4**.

Continue twining until the base measures 10" across or until there is space between all the spokes to add the 1/4" spokes. As in **Diagram 5**, lay the 1/4" spokes (oval side down) and twine around them on the center mark as you come to the spaces. Leave half the piece free and extended toward the center of the base. The pieces in the center of the base may be cumbersome for a little while but it is only temporary. When all 24 stakes are added, twine around 2 more times.

Now fold the extended half of the spoke over on itself and match the ends. See **Diagram 6**. The 2 thick-

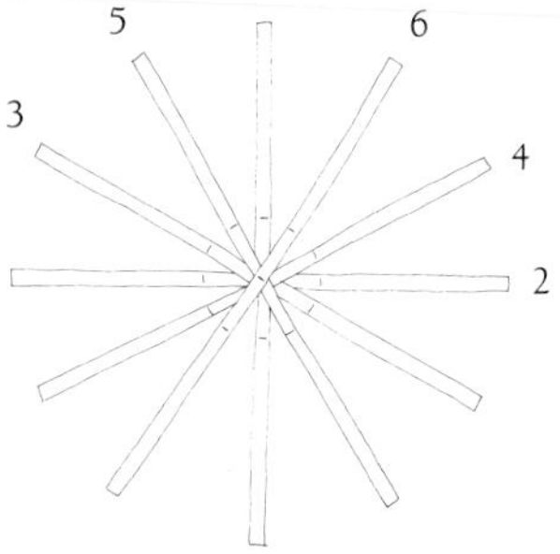

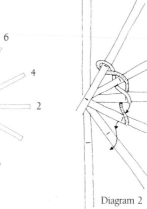

Diagram 1

Diagram 2

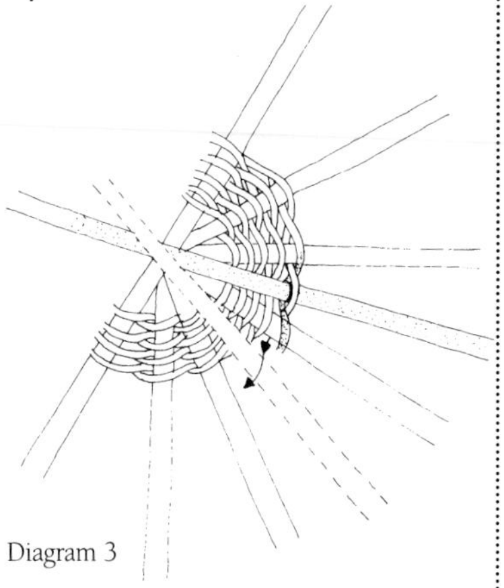

Diagram 3

nesses are treated as one. Twine for 4 more rows with the spokes folded. The base should now measure 12" in diameter. End and tuck the weavers as in **Diagram 7**.

WEAVING THE SIDES

Turn the base over so the smooth side of the reed is facing up. Place 4 pieces of #3 round reed behind any 4 consecutive spokes. As in **Diagram 8**, do 1 row of 4-rod wale, always picking up the weaver farthest left and taking it to the right over 3, behind 1 and to the outside of the basket.

After 1 row is completed, cut the farthest left piece of #3 round reed and upsett the spokes. With the sides now standing, do 5 rows of 3-rod wale. In 3-rod wale, use the farthest left weaver each stroke and weave it to the right over 2 spokes, behind 1 and to the outside of the basket. See **Diagram 9**. End the 3-rod wale by cutting each piece behind

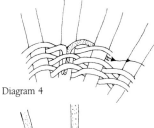

Diagram 4

Diagram 5

Diagram 6

Diagram 7

Diagram 8

Diagram 9

the 3 spokes just before the beginning spokes.

The following color sequence is used to make the decorative arrow design: green, peach, wine, tan.

Insert a piece of green 1/4" flat oval reed so it is behind 1 spoke and angled slightly to the right. Weave it over 1, under 1, over 2 and let it rest to the inside. See **Diagram 10**.

Next, insert a piece of peach 1/4" flat oval reed in the same manner, placing it behind the spoke to the left of the green weaver. See **Diagram 11**. Continue adding pieces, each time to the left of the spoke before, keeping the color sequence, and weaving to the right until all

48 pieces are in place. *Note:* You may find it easier to insert the last 2 pieces from the right in the appropriate places. See **Diagram 12**. Pack all the weavers down very tightly. Cut each weaver just beyond the spoke it is resting behind. See **Diagram 13**. Do not discard the remains of these spokes. They are used to make the top half of the arrow.

Now weave the top half of the arrow pattern. Match colors as you insert pieces. Using the pieces that remained after cutting, begin behind any spoke with the same color that ended behind that spoke. This time, weave to the left and angle the pieces upward.

Weave over 2, under 1, over 1 and to the inside of the basket. See **Diagram 14**. Continue adding pieces to the right and weaving them to the left. When all 48 weavers are in place, pack all of them down snugly. Cut off any excess and make sure the end of each piece is behind a spoke.

Starting anywhere with 3 long soaked #3 round reed weavers, work 3 rows of 3-rod wale. Refer to **Diagram 15** for how to do 3-rod wale. End waling as before.

Next, weave one start-stop row with a soaked piece of 3/8" flat reed, beginning on top of a 1/4" flat oval spoke. Begin and end the row as in **Diagram 16**. The

1/4" flat oval spokes should be on the inside of the last row of weaving, with the 1/2" spokes being on the outside. Cut all the 1/4" spokes flush with the top of the row of 3/8" flat reed. Point all the 1/2" spokes, soak them and bend them to the inside over the row of 3/8" flat. Tuck them behind the first available row of weaving. See **Diagram 16**.

FINISHING

Insert the 2 handles on the inside of the basket under 1 row of weaving, making the notch lie on top of the rim row of 3/8" flat. There should be 2 spokes between the handle span. There should be 20 spokes

Outside

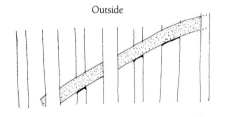

Diagram 10

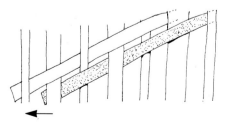

Diagram 11

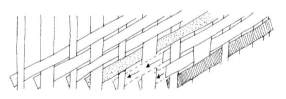

Diagram 12

Inside view

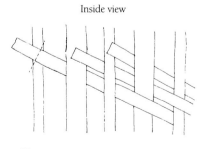

Diagram 13

between the 2 handles to make them evenly spaced. See **Diagram 17**.

Soak 2 pieces of 1/2" flat oval reed, each long enough to reach around the rim and overlap 3" to 4". When soaked, place 1 piece around the outside, covering the 3/8" row, holding it in place with clothespins. Shave both the ends where they overlap so the thickness of the overlapped area is no greater than a single thickness of reed. Repeat the procedure with the other piece of 1/2" flat oval reed on the inside of the rim. Hold both pieces in place with clothespins.

Lay a piece of #6 round reed on top of and between the 2 pieces of rim. This #6 round reed is a filler and hides the ends of the spokes. Let the ends overlap for 2" or 3". Bevel the ends so the area of overlap is no thicker than a single piece of round reed and looks like one continuous piece.

Lash all the pieces together with a long piece of soaked cane. "Lose" the lasher by hooking it over the basket wall, going up under the inside rim, over the wall and down under the outside rim. See **Diagram 18** for rims and lashing. Insert the lasher into every space between spokes just under the rim. End the lasher as begun or hide it under a weaver.

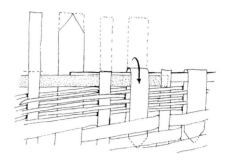

Diagram 16

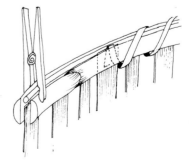

Diagram 17

Outside view

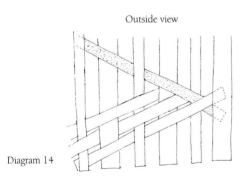

Diagram 14

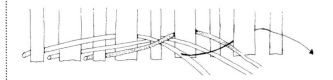

Diagram 15

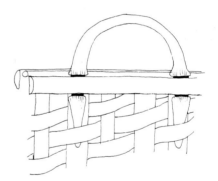

Diagram 18

Inspired by a Pueblo basket and designed to sit on the floor, this basket could be used to hold umbrellas or long-stemmed flowers. It is nice and decorative, however, just left empty.

APPROXIMATE SIZE
15" diameter x 15" high

MATERIALS NEEDED
1/2" flat reed (spokes)
1/4" flat oval reed (weavers)
11/64" flat reed (weavers)
1/2" maple strips (curls)

Pueblo Vase

PRELIMINARY STEP
Dye 4 long pieces of 1/2" flat reed with turquoise dye and 2 long pieces with peach dye. Each of the 6 pieces should be at least 55" long.

WEAVING THE BASE
From the natural 1/2" flat reed, cut 16 pieces 45" long. Soak all the pieces several minutes or until pliable. In pencil, mark a center on the rough side of all the pieces. Also, on 8 of the pieces, mark 1-1/2" on each side of the center mark. See **Diagram 1**. As in **Diagram 1**, lay the 8 marked pieces like spokes in a wheel, wrong side up, matching center marks. Starting with one vertical piece, lay the others so they alternate directions as in the diagram. The weaving on the base is referred to as an Indian weave.

With a long piece of soaked 11/64" flat reed, begin on top of any spoke on the 1-1/2" mark and continue under the next, over the

next, etc., keeping the weaver on or outside the 1-1/2" mark. When the starting spoke is reached, weave over the "beginning tail" to the fourth spoke. Instead of continuing over the fifth spoke, weave over both fifth and sixth spokes. This jump over 2 spokes puts the weaver in a different path, going under and over alternately. Weave 10 rows of Indian weave or until there is ample room for another spoke to fit between the existing spokes. See **Diagram 2**. End the weaving by cutting it behind the fourth spoke when the tenth row is complete rather than jumping the next 2 spokes and continuing. See **Diagram 3**. Lay the other 8 spokes in the spaces and begin weaving again with a long piece of 11/64" flat as before. Weave 6 more rows in the Indian weave. End weaver as before. See **Diagram 4**.

With a soaked, 1/4" flat oval reed, begin weaving

start-stop rows, as in **Diagram 5**, putting the oval side of the reed on the bottom of the base. If the flat oval reed is very thick, shave some of the thickness from the ends where they overlap. Overlap each row 4 spokes as in **Diagram 6**. The rest of the base is woven in start-stop rows with the base still flat on a table until the diameter is approximately 10".

WEAVING THE SIDES
Begin to tighten very gradually on the weaver so the sides slowly begin to stand. After 4 or 5 rows of tightening on the weaver, the sides should be rounding upward. See **Diagram 7**.

You must keep a close eye on the diameter of the basket once the sides begin to stand. The fullest point of the basket is where the color rows are woven in. At this time the diameter should be about 14". The pattern of widths and colors on the sides of the basket is:

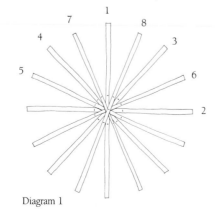

Diagram 1

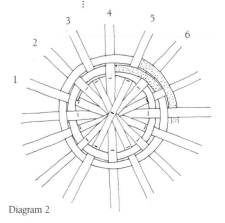

Diagram 2

- Weave 10 rows of natural 1/4" flat oval.
- Weave 1 row of 1/2" flat reed dyed peach.
- Weave 1 row of 1/2" flat reed dyed turquoise.
- Weave 1 row of natural 11/64" flat reed.
- Weave 1 row of 1/2" flat reed dyed turquoise.
- Weave 1 row of 1/2" flat reed dyed peach.

Weave 16 rows of 1/4" flat oval reed. Now you should press in on the spokes and gradually pull tighter on the weaver so the sides begin to lean in and the circumference of the basket becomes smaller. See **Diagram 8**.

At the smallest point, after the 16 rows of flat oval, the neck of the basket should be approximately 9-1/2" in diameter. Weave in 2 rows of 1/2" dyed turquoise. Again return to the 1/4" flat oval and begin to make the top of the basket flare. Gently at first, weave from the inside of the basket and press outward on the spokes. Weave 3 rows of natural 1/4" flat oval. At this point, soak the ends of the spokes as far down as the last row of weaving. Cut every spoke lengthwise as nearly in the middle as possible to the last row of weaving. See **Diagram 8**.

Resume weaving with the natural 1/4" flat oval reed. Weave from the inside of the basket and push out on the spokes to make them flare. Weave with the oval side of the reed on the inside of the basket now. *Note:* If you can't get the extremely flared shape you want, place the wet basket upside down (sitting on the spokes) on a flat surface. Press down on the basket, making the spokes' flare greatly exaggerated. Place a heavy object on the basket base, pushing the spokes outward even more. Make the spokes flare even more than you ultimately want them to, as they will invariably be pressed in as

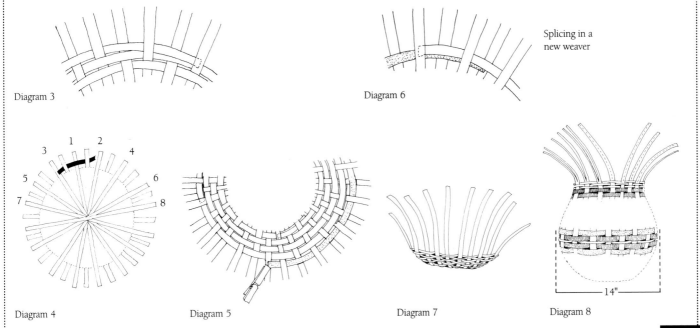

Diagram 3

Diagram 6

Splicing in a new weaver

Diagram 4

Diagram 5

Diagram 7

Diagram 8

14"

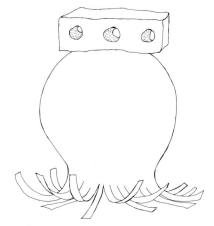

Diagram 9

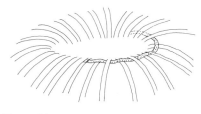

Diagram 10

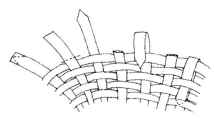

Diagram 11

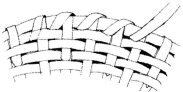

Diagram 12

you weave. Let the spokes dry in place. See **Diagram 9**. Continue to weave for 15 or 16 more rows with the spokes flaring outward as in **Diagram 10**.

FINISHING THE BASKET

Point all the stakes on the inside of the basket. Cut all the spokes on the outside flush with the last row of weaving. Soak the ends again, bend the pointed spokes over the last row of weaving and tuck them behind the first available row of weaving on the inside of the basket. See **Diagram 11**.

Soak a long piece of 1/4" flat oval and lash, as in **Diagram 12**, through every space. Tuck the end into the weaving on the outside of the basket.

MAKE CURLS & FOOT

Two rows of curls are inserted over the 4 rows of colored 1/2" flat reed in the center of the basket and 1 row over the 2 colored rows at the

neck. See **Diagram 13** for placement.

Soak a long piece of 1/2" maple and begin as in **Diagram 14** by inserting one end behind a spoke on the bottom colored row. Loop the piece around and, keeping the wrong side up, move behind the next spoke on the top row. Continue looping the maple and alternating top and bottom rows, taking it behind each stake. Add a piece if necessary by ending the old one and starting the new one behind the same spoke. **Diagram 15** shows the 2 rows of curls.

To make the "foot" on the bottom of the basket, soak a long piece of 11/64" flat or flat oval reed. Fold it in half and crisscross under every spoke as in **Diagram 16**. The piece of reed goes under the 11/64" with which the bottom was woven. End where it began by tucking the ends under the "x" and trace for 2 "stitches" to keep it from pulling out.

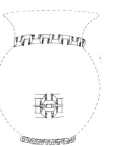

Diagram 13

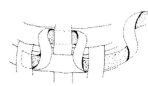

Diagram 14

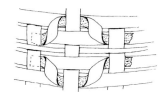

Diagram 15

Diagram 16

VICTORIAN

Daisy Shopper

This lovely shopper was designed by Debbie Richards of Lake Orion, Michigan. It fits comfortably on the arm for shopping and decorates any room when not going to or from the market. Several weaving techniques are employed, including continuous twill weave, four-rod arrow and a braided border.

APPROXIMATE SIZE
11" x 14" x 14" high

MATERIALS
7mm flat oval or 1/4" flat oval
  (thin and flexible weavers)
5/8" flat reed (stakes)
#2 round reed (arrow and
  border)
1-1/2" ash, poplar or maple
  (decorative strip)
#0 or #1 round reed
  (twining around base)
7" x 14" Williamsburg handle
Dark green (hunter) dye

PRELIMINARY STEP
From the 5/8" flat reed, cut 10 pieces 36" long and 14 pieces 32" long. Soak all the pieces until they are pliable. Mark the centers of all the pieces on the wrong (rough) side.

WEAVING THE BASE
To weave the base, lay the ten 36" pieces horizontally with all the pieces flush together (no space between pieces), wrong side up. Approximately 6" to the left of the center marks, begin weaving the 32" pieces in vertically in the following pattern:

o=Over   u=Under
Row 1: o2, u2, o2, u2, o2. See **Diagram 1**.
Row 2: u1, o2, u2, o2, u2, o1.
Row 3: u2, o2, u2, o2, u2.
Row 4: o1, u2, o2, u2, o2, u1.
Row 5: Repeat Row 1.
Row 6: Repeat Row 2.
Row 7: Repeat Row 3.
Row 8: Weave in handle as a stake in the Row 4 pattern.
Row 9-Row 14: Repeat Rows 1-4 until the last piece has been woven. See **Diagram 2** (Arrow shows where next one will go.)

Measure and true the base to approximately 7" x 11". With a soaked piece of #0 or #1 round reed, twine around the base as in **Diagram 3**. Fold the weaver in half and begin twining by looping the fold around a stake. End the twining by pushing the end under itself at the beginning.

Cut all 8 of the corner stakes in half from the end of the piece to the woven base. This will allow the corners to flare. See **Diagram 3**.

Upsett all the stakes by bending them over upon themselves at the base. They won't stand permanently, but the crease is necessary. See **Diagram 3A**.

WEAVING THE SIDES
Soak a long piece of 1/4" flat oval or 7mm flat oval reed until it is very pliable. Taper one end for approximately 12" so it is about 1/8" at the very end and gradually widens to 1/4". Begin anywhere and weave over 2 stakes and under 1 around the basket. When the starting point is reached, continue in the weaving pattern; the "over 2" will move over 1 stake and a twill pattern will emerge. See **Diagram 4**.

Note: Should you want to try this weave using a different number of stakes, in

Diagram 1

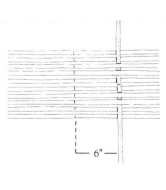

Diagram 2

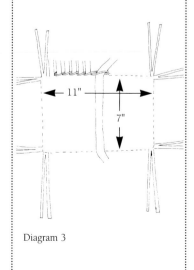

Diagram 3

Diagram 3a

Diagram 4

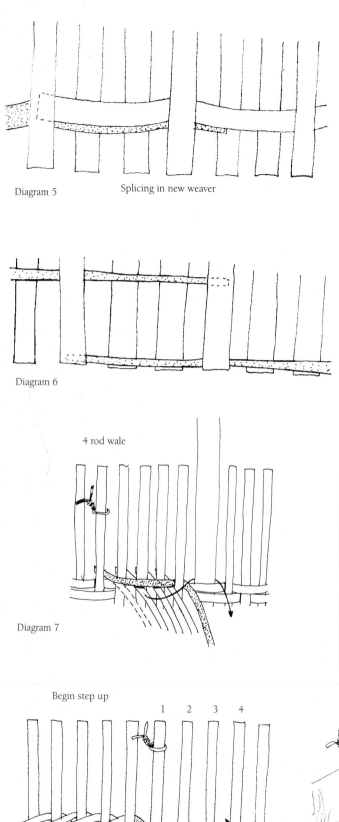

Diagram 5   Splicing in new weaver

Diagram 6

4 rod wale

Diagram 7

order for the pattern to work, the total number of stakes used must be a number that is divisible by 3, plus or minus 1. In this basket the total number of stakes is 56, which is divisible by 3 (57) minus 1 (56).

Continue weaving around the basket for 15 rows. Be sure to watch the corners closely to make them flare and not let them pull in too much. Add a weaver when one runs out, as in **Diagram 5**, by starting a new one behind the fourth stake before the end of the old one, weaving with the 2 weavers for 4 stakes. Directly above the place you started weaving, taper the end of the weaver again down to 1/8". End the weaver above where you started. See **Diagram 6**.

ARROW WEAVE

If you have problems with the arrow weave, see a more detailed explanation in "Up Close."

Using 2 long soaked pieces of natural #2 round reed and 2 long soaked pieces of dyed #2 round reed, work one row of 4-rod wale. Begin, as in **Diagram 7**, by placing the 4 pieces behind 4 consecutive stakes in the following sequence:

■ 1 natural
■ 1 dyed
■ 1 natural
■ 1 dyed

Mark the stake behind which you place the first weaver. (The starting stake is marked in **Diagram 7** with a twist-tie.)

Begin with the farthest left (natural) weaver. Weave it over 3 stakes, behind 1 and to the outside. See **Diagram 7**. Repeat with the other 3 and continue repeating the 4 strokes around the basket. When the lead weaver is one stake before the marked one, work a "step-up" to complete 1 row. To do a step-up, move the first (right) weaver in front of 3 and behind the fourth. See **Diagram 8**. Next move the second (to the left) weaver over 3 and behind 1 and to the outside. Repeat with the other 2 weavers in succession.

Continuing to make the arrow weave pattern, do 1 row of reverse 4-rod wale. Again, as in the 4-rod wale, use the farthest left weaver, move it over 3 stakes to the right, behind the fourth and to the outside, but be sure the weaver moves under the other 3 instead of over them as in a regular 4 rod wale. See **Diagram 9**. Stop the

Begin step up

1   2   3   4

Diagram 8

Starting arrow

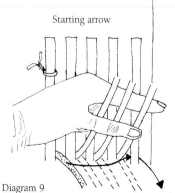

Diagram 9

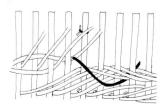

Diagram 10

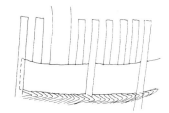

Diagram 11

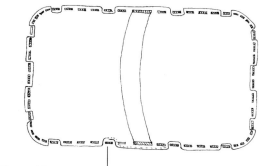

Diagram 12

Begin here (overlap on dotted line to finish)

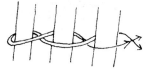

Diagram 13

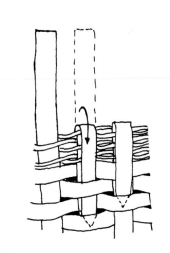

Diagram 14

reverse 4-rod wale behind the stake immediately before the starting stake.

End by "locking" the 4-rod arrow in the following manner: Using the "farthest right" weaver, move it over 3 stakes to the right and under the 3 rows of weaving already in place and behind the fourth stake to be cut later. Again, using the farthest right weaver, move it to the right, over 3 stakes and under the 3 rows of weaving already in place and behind the fourth stake to be cut later. Repeat with the other 2 weavers, ending the last weaver behind the starting stake. See **Diagram 10**.

WEAVING IN THE ROW OF ASH
Looking at **Diagram 11** and using either long side of the basket, start the weaver behind the second stake to the left of the handle. Weave the soaked piece of ash, as in

Diagram 12, overlapping the beginning and ending for 4 stakes. *Note:* Some are over 2 and some are over 3, and corners are under 4. Be aware of the irregularity of the weave and watch **Diagram 12** closely.

CONTINUE WEAVING THE SIDES
Repeat the row of 4-rod wale, the step-up and the row of reverse 4-rod wale ending as before to create another row of arrow weave.

Again, taper a soaked piece of flat oval weaving material for several inches and begin again weaving around the basket in an over 2 and under 1 weave. Weave 4 more rows. End the weaver by tapering it, as in the beginning, directly above the spot it began. Refer to **Diagram 6**.

Soak a long piece of #2 round reed. Fold it in half and twine around the stakes for 3 rows. See **Diagram 13**.

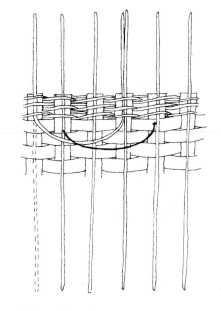

Diagram 15

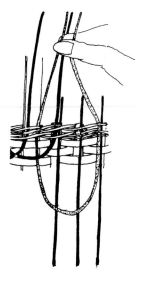

Diagram 16

End the twining directly above the place it began by tucking the ends into the weaving.

FINISHING THE STAKES & MAKING THE BORDER

Point all the stakes, as in **Diagram 14**, and after they are rewet, bend them over to the inside of the basket and tuck them into the weaving so the ends are hidden behind a weaver.

Soak all the 36" pieces of dyed #2 round reed. When they are pliable, insert all the pieces under the 3 rows of natural twining on the outside, as in **Diagram 15**. Leave a tail that is little more than half the length of the piece extended below the twining. Now, form scallops by taking each tail over 2 stakes to the right and inserting it upward under the twining on the third stake. Hold both the tails of each piece and pull them up until the scallop is placed evenly under the twining.

See **Diagram 16**.

BRAIDED BORDER:
Take any pair of stakes behind the pair to its right and to the outside. Continue with each pair around the basket. See **Diagram 17**. End the row, as in **Diagram 18**, by pushing the last pair behind the beginning pair.

Starting anywhere again, move one pair of stakes over the 3 pairs to its right and to the inside of the basket, going *under the ends of the 3 stakes*. See **Diagram 19**. End the row, as in **Diagram 20**, moving the last pair over the 3 stakes with which the row began to the inside of the basket.

To finish the border, do a simple rolled border on the inside of the basket. Working from the inside of the basket, take any pair over the 2 pairs to its right and down to the inside. See **Diagram 21**. End by moving the last pair over 2 and behind the beginning pair. See **Diagram 22**. Repeat the rolled border 4 or more times.

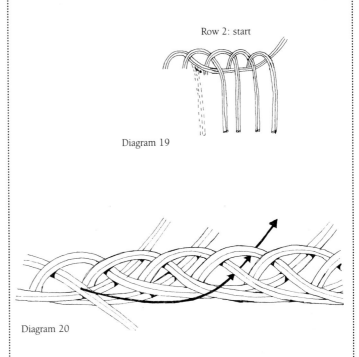

Row 2: start

Diagram 19

Diagram 20

Rolled border start

Diagram 21

Beginning braided border

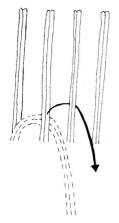

Diagram 17

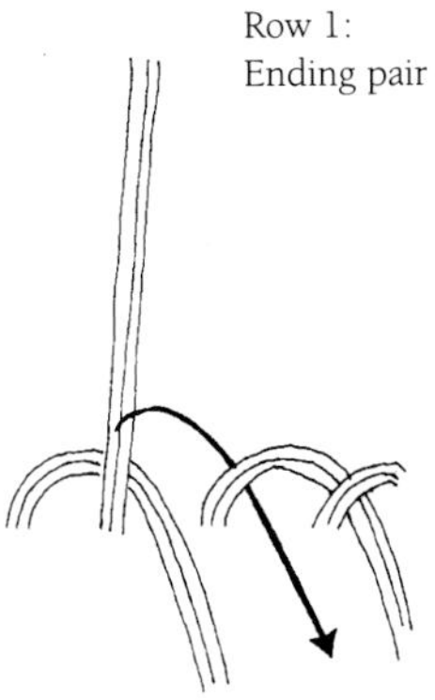

Row 1: Ending pair

Diagram 18

Rolled border end

Diagram 22

Victorian Flower Stand

Mark Katz of LaFarge, Wisconsin, whose specialty is willow and round reed, designed this pattern after studying many antique flower stands. He has made every effort to retain authenticity in each detail of construction. What truly Victorian parlor can be complete without one!

APPROXIMATE SIZE

24" diameter x 34" high

MATERIALS

3/16" flat oval reed (weavers)
#5 round reed (spokes)
#2 round reed (weavers)
#3 round reed (weavers)
#8 round reed (handle)
#12 round reed (handle)
3/4" x #18 wire nails
1" dowel
2" x 6" x 18" board
1/2" x 3" diameter wood disk

PRELIMINARY STEP

It may be possible to construct this basket without this stand that Mark designed, but it surely is an invaluable aid.

As in **Diagram 1**, cut a 1" diameter dowel 38" long. Cut a base from the 2" x 6" lumber that is 18" long. Connect the 2 pieces with a wood screw, going into the 2"x 6" piece first, then into the dowel.

Cut a disk from the 1/2" thick wood that is 3" in diameter. Tack the base onto the end of the dowel.

MAKING THE FOOT

From the #5 round reed, cut 23 pieces 48" long. Make a mark on the pieces 12" from one end.

Make 23 marks on the 3" disk that are fairly equidistant.

Nail the pieces onto the disk as in **Diagram 2**, with the 3/4" x #18 nails, driving them through the 12" mark on the round reed. See **Diagram 3** for a bird's-eye view of the disk with the spokes nailed into it. The longer ends of the spokes will be left freely hanging as in **Diagram 4**.

As in **Diagram 5**, begin twining around the spokes by folding a soaked #2 round reed almost in half. Take the top piece under the next spoke each stroke. See "Up Close and Technical" if you need additional help with twining. Twine around the spokes from the inside for 5", making the spokes flare from the very begin-

ning. When you have twined for 5", the diameter should be approximately 10". Add on a new weaver when necessary, as in **Diagram 6**, laying the new one beside the old one and letting the ends overlap for about 1". Ends can be cut later to "butt". End the twining as in **Diagram 7** by pushing the ends into the twined area with 2 consecutive spokes.

Make a finishing border by bringing each spoke in front of the spoke to the right and to the inside. See **Diagram 8**.

MAKING THE VASE SECTION

As shown in **Diagram 9**, the basket can now be removed from the stand and will sit on the woven foot.

Soak a piece of 3/16" flat oval reed until it is pliable. Taper the end for 4" to 6" to about half its width. Begin weaving around the spokes, coming up the sides as in

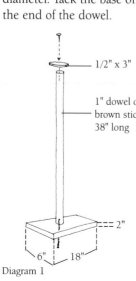

1/2" x 3"

1" dowel or brown stick 38" long

2"

6"   18"

Diagram 1

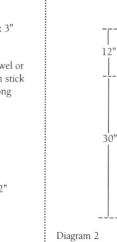

12"   Base

30"

Diagram 2

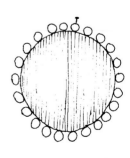

Cross section with all spokes nailed on

Diagram 3

Diagram 10. The weaving is continuous. Add on a 3/16" flat oval weaver when one runs out as in **Diagram 11**, shaving some of the thickness from the overlapped area if necessary. Gradually flare the sides all the way, keeping in mind that after 10" of weaving, the diameter of the opening should be approximately 8".

End the 3/16" flat oval weaver after 10" of weaving by tapering the end for several inches and letting it just run out. End the weaver above the point where you started. See **Diagram 12**.

After 10" of weaving, the shape must flare drastically.

Cut 8 pieces of #5 round reed 16" long. Slype the ends (cut at an angle) of the 8 new spokes and push the slyped ends into the weaving beside an existing spoke. To space them equidistantly, start anywhere and place a new spoke with every third

Diagram 4

Diagram 5

Diagram 6

Old weaver   New weaver

Diagram 7

Diagram 8

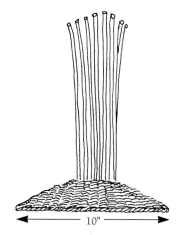

|← 10" →|

Diagram 9

spoke except the last one which must be placed with the second spoke over. See **Diagram 13** for spacing. Push the new ones 2" to 3" into the existing weaving as in **Diagram 14** (**Diagram 15** shows a detailed view). Begin twining again by folding a soaked #3 round reed weaver almost in half. Take one end under one spoke and the other end under the next. See **Diagram 16**. Weave from the inside, causing the shape to flare drastically. After 3-1/2" of twining, tuck the ends into the weaving to end the twining. At this point, the diameter of the opening should be approximately 15".

MAKING THE BORDER

Starting with any spoke, take it behind the one to the right and to the outside. Each spoke does the same in its turn. The last standing spoke goes behind the first one that is already in place. The arrow demonstrates the path it should take. See **Diagram 17**.

Then take each spoke over 2 spokes to the right to the inside, going under the ends of the other spokes. See **Diagram 18**. The arrow shows the last 2 spokes going into place. See **Diagram 19**.

Last, bring each spoke behind 1 and to the outside, where it will be cut later. See **Diagram 20**.

Starting tapered weaver

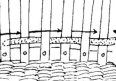

Diagram 10

Ending tapered weaver

Diagram 12

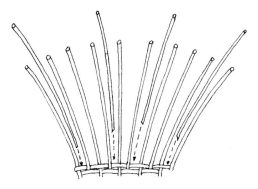

Diagram 14

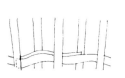

Diagram 11

Diagram 13

Diagram 15

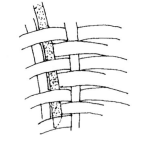

Diagram 16

MAKING &
ATTACHING THE HANDLE

From the #12 round reed, cut a piece 84" long. Shave the ends for 1-1/2" so they are very thin at the ends. Soak the piece until it is pliable. Also cut and soak 2 pieces of #8 round reed that are each at least 72" long. Push the ends of the #12 round reed into the sides of the basket at the base, pushing them through the twiing and making them lie flat against the sides of the disk. See **Diagram 21**. Nail the handle into the disk on both sides. Count the spokes on each side and place the handle so it is equidistant. See

Diagram 22.

Insert the ends of the #8 round reed into the sides of the basket at the top, going under the border. Wrap both ends, making X's as you go, as in **Diagram 22**. Push the ends into the other side the same way you began.

With a soaked piece of 3/8" flat reed, make 1 complete wrap around the base, going over the disk and over the handle. Overlap the ends 1" to 2" and nail in place. See **Diagram 23**.

Since this basket has traditionally been painted white, you can paint it with a semigloss latex enamel if you so desire.

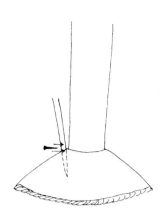

Diagram 21

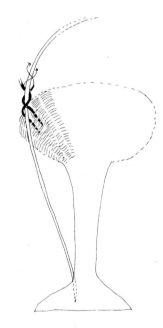

Diagram 22

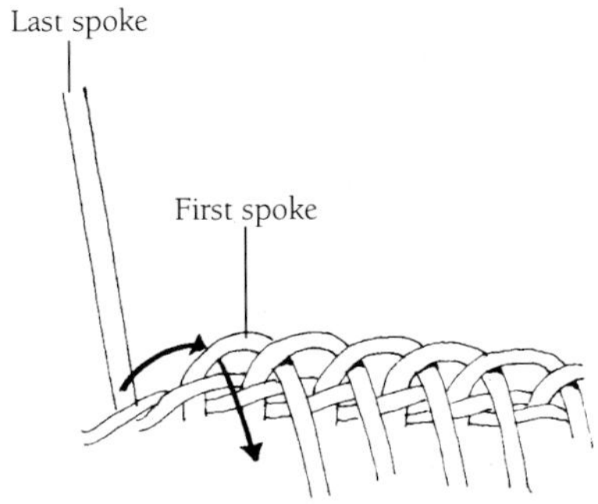

Last spoke

First spoke

Diagram 17

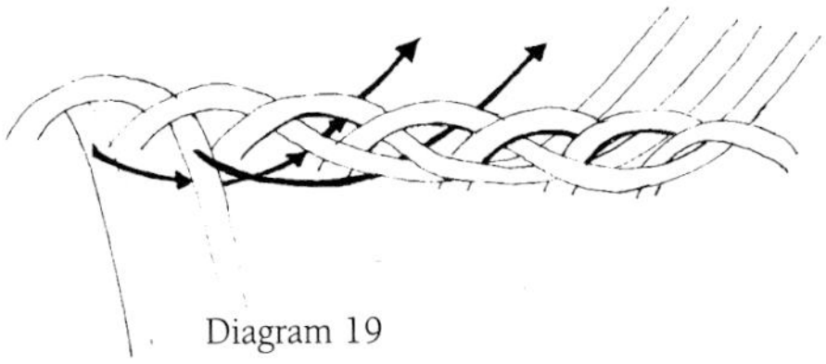

Diagram 19

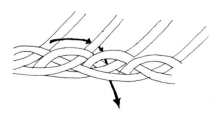

Diagram 18

Diagram 20

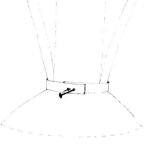

Diagram 23

Victorian Vanity Basket

This wonderful basket was designed by Genie Jackson of Coral Springs, Florida. Use it in any Victorian room. Fill it with hand towels or toiletries on your vanity. Line it with a matching fabric or lace so it can hold smaller items.

APPROXIMATE SIZE
7-1/2" x 12-1/2" x 8" high

MATERIALS
1/4" or 7mm flat oval reed
   (weaver and stake)
1" ash (weaver)
#2 round reed (weavers
   and border)
3/8" flat reed (stakes)
3/8" half round reed (runners)
Medium chair cane (lacing)
8" x 8" wood D handle

PRELIMINARY STEP
Dye approximately 1/3 hank of #2 round reed rose pink. Cut 36 pieces 40"long for the border. Five or 6 long dyed pieces are used for the arrow weave around the sides of the basket also.

CUTTING THE STAKES
From the 3/8" flat reed cut 3 pieces 27" long and 8 pieces 22" long. Mark the centers on the rough side. From the 1/4" flat oval reed cut 6 pieces 27" long and 6 pieces 22" long. Again mark the centers on the rough side.

WEAVING THE BASE
Soak all the stakes until they are pliable, along with 3 or 4 long pieces of natural #2 round reed. In pencil, mark the center of the handle on the inside bottom. Also, mark 3-3/8" to either side of the center mark. See **Diagram 1**. Place the handle vertically on a flat surface. Alternating the stakes over and under the handle, beginning at the top of the handle, lay the following stakes:

■ Three 27" long 1/4" flat oval stakes
■ Three 27" long 3/8" flat stakes
■ Three 27" long 1/4" flat oval stakes

Lay all pieces rough side up. The measurement from the first to the last stake should be approximately 6-3/4". See **Diagram 2**.

On each side of the handle weave four 22" (3/8") flat stakes, then three 22" (1/4") flat oval stakes, all with the rough side up. The base should measure 6-3/4" x 11-3/4". See **Diagram 3**.

Turn the base over for the moment and measure 2 pieces of 3/8" half round so the ends will fit smoothly over the 3/8" stakes. Measure in from each end about 3/8" on the half round and mark. With a knife or small hacksaw, cut on the mark from the rounded side halfway through the reed. Scoop out the reed between the two cuts. Place the half round runners on top of the third 3/8" stake from the handle in each direction with the notches under the edge horizontal stakes. See **Diagram 4**. Runners will be laced in place later.

Turn the base back to "wrong side up." Referring to **Diagram 3**, mark the corners, as shown on the base. Begin twining as in **Diagram 5**. The twining will not go to the corner of the woven base, but rather will go diagonally across, as in **Diagram 6**, on the diagonal mark you made. Twine 2 rows around the base, following the pattern lines at the corners. You will be twining over the "X"

Center

3-3/8"

3-3/8"

Diagram 1

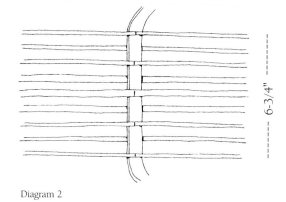

6-3/4"

Diagram 2

of 2 stakes as in **Diagram 6**. End twining by tucking the ends into the twined area beside a stake.

UPSETTING & WEAVING THE SIDES

Rewet the stakes with a spray bottle or sponge and upsett them as in **Diagram 7**. Bend every stake over on itself toward the inside of the base. Weave 4 start-stop rows with 1/4" natural flat oval reed. End each row by overlapping 4 stakes. See **Diagrams 8 & 8A**. You will treat the double stakes on the diagonal as one. See **Diagram 9**.

Make a row of pairing arrow, using 2 pieces of dyed #2 round reed. As in **Diagram 10**, twine 1 row around the basket. When you return to the starting point, reverse twine around the basket for 1 row. Reverse twine by lifting the weaver on the right and taking the left weaver under the right, behind the stake and back to

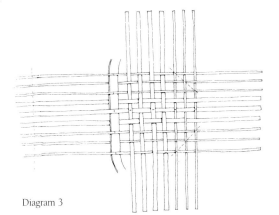

Diagram 3

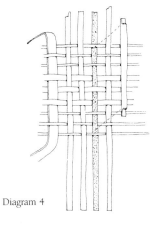

Diagram 4

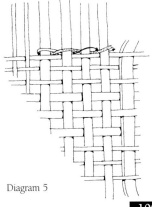

Diagram 5

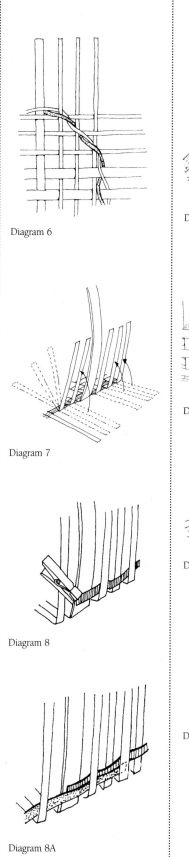

Diagram 6

Diagram 7

Diagram 8

Diagram 8A

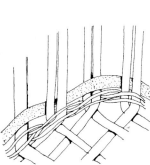

Diagram 9

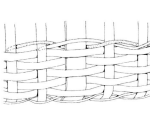

Diagram 10

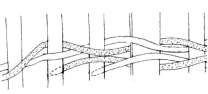

Diagram 11

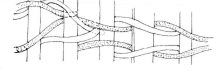

Diagram 12

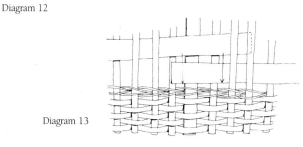

Diagram 13

the outside of the basket. See **Diagram 11**.

End the arrow pattern by tucking the weaver under the beginning of the second row. See **Diagram 12**. Weave in 1 row of 1" ash, starting on the stake to the left of the handle and going over 3, under 2, over 2, under 2, over 3, under 2, over 2, under 2; repeat. Overlap the ends of the ash 4 stakes. See **Diagram 13**.

Weave another pairing arrow with the dyed #2 round reed. Weave 3 start-stop, over 1, under 1 rows of 1/4" flat oval. Twine 3 rows with #2 natural round reed. End twining by tucking the ends down into the twined area beside a stake. Point every stake and tuck it behind a row of weaving as in **Diagram 14**.

MAKING THE REWOVEN BORDER

Soak the 36 pieces of #2 dyed round reed. Insert all the pieces under the 3 rows of natural twining as in the first stakes in **Diagram 15**. Leave a "tail" that is a little more than half the piece extended below the

twining. Now form scallops by taking each "tail" over 1 stake to the right and inserting it upward under the twining on the second stake. Make sure ends and scallops are even. See **Diagram 15**. Pieces of reed are now in pairs.

Rewet ends of reed if they have dried any. Start with any pair of spokes and take it behind the pair to the right and out. See **Diagram 16**. Repeat all the way around the rim. End row by pushing the last pair under the already bent "first pair." See **Diagram 17**.

Next, take any pair under the pair to the right and up without going inside the basket. See **Diagram 18**. Weave these 2 rows rather loosely so it is easier to weave in the next step. See **Diagram 19**. Next, each spoke must trace the path of the spoke to its right. First it will tuck underneath the braid to the outside. It will then follow the braid and tuck to the inside. See **Diagram 20**.

These 3 rows will be on the outside of the handle. The last 2 will be on the inside and are a simple rolled border over 2 pairs of spokes and down to the inside of

Inside view

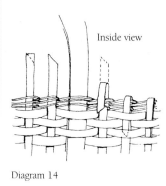

Diagram 14

the basket. See **Diagram 21**.
Each row is ended when you
have 2 pairs remaining. To
find where to tuck the far
left pair, push up on the
beginning pair. Again bring
the far left pair to the right
and tuck into the loop
formed by pushing up the
beginning pair. Now, push
up the second pair and tuck
the remaining pair into the
loop formed nearest the basket. Repeat this tucking at
the end of the second row of
the rolled border. Cut spokes
to 1-1/2" and dry.

With a piece of medium
chair cane, lace each runner
in place. Find the center of
the piece of cane and wrap it
around the runner from the
inside to the outside. The
ends of the cane should be
coming out between the first
row of twining and the edge
stake. Start with one end of
cane and lace downward
around each stake and the
runner to the opposite side
of the base. With the other
end of the cane, again lace
on a slant to the opposite
side of the base, forming an
X pattern. See **Diagram 22**.
Tuck cane ends so they are
hidden and secure. See **Diagram 23**.

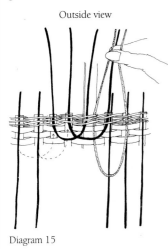

Outside view

Diagram 15

PAINTING INSTRUCTIONS FOR FORGET-ME-NOT HEARTS
By Jeanine Gonzalez

SUPPLIES NEEDED
Acrylic Paint
- ■ Green
- ■ Rust
- ■ Blue
- ■ Yellow
- ■ Raspberry
- ■ Purple
- ■ Synthetic brushes (#2 flat and liner)

The flowers need not be
traced onto your surface. Simply place a dot with a pencil
to indicate the flower center.
Each flower has 5 petals. Use
the small flat brush and rotate
on one corner to create each
petal. Paint the flowers using
purple, raspberry and blue.
The flower centers are dotted
in with the corner of the small
flat brush or a stylus, using
yellow with rust to shade.
Place some leaves, using the
small flat brush and green.
The stems and line work are
green.

The hearts are done with
raspberry. Using the brush
handle, place 2 round dots
of paint side by side. Using
the liner brush, pull the
paint downward to connect
the dots to the bottom to
form a heart. Place 3 dots of
raspberry below the heart.

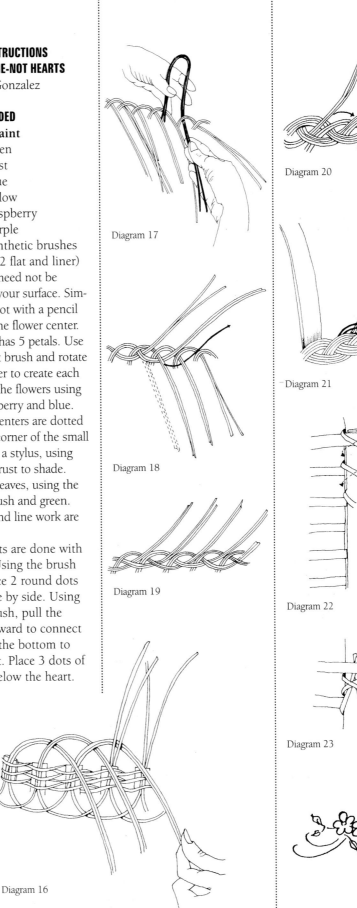

Diagram 16

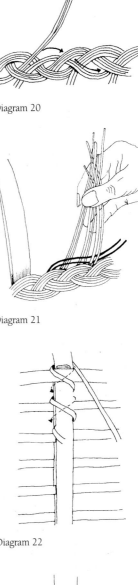

Diagram 17

Diagram 18

Diagram 19

Diagram 20

Diagram 21

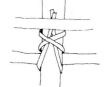

Diagram 22

Diagram 23

English Shopper

APPROXIMATE SIZE
6" x 13" x 16" high

MATERIALS NEEDED
5/8" flat reed (weavers)
5/8" flat reed, smoked or dyed
   brown (weavers)
3/8" flat reed (filler strips and
   weavers)
1/4" flat reed (stakes,
   weavers and flowers)
#4 round reed (border)
#3 round reed (twining)
2 large bushel basket handles
Green, rose and brown dye
   (if you are dying reed
   instead of using smoked
   reed).

PRELIMINARY STEP
Dye enough 1/4" flat reed for the stakes and several pieces of 3/8" flat reed for leaves green. Dye several long pieces of 1/4" flat reed rose for the flowers. Dye 5 long pieces of 5/8" flat reed brown for the ground if you do not have smoked reed.

WEAVING THE BASE
From the 1/4" flat green reed, cut 10 pieces 40" long. From the 5/8" flat natural reed, cut 10 pieces 40" long. From the 3/8" flat natural reed, cut 6 pieces 26" long.

Soak all the pieces until they are pliable. Mark the centers of all the pieces on the wrong (rough) side. Aligning the center marks, lay the pieces horizontally as in **Diagram 1**, wrong side up. Starting on one side, lay a 1/4" flat green, a 3/8" flat natural, a 5/8" flat natural and a 3/8" flat natural. Repeat the sequence 2 more times and finally lay a 1/4" flat green. There are 13 horizontal stakes.

Weave a 5/8" flat (natural) piece wrong side up, vertically, in an over 1, under 1 pattern. Place it on the center marks of the horizontal pieces. See **Diagram 1**. Be sure the 5/8" piece goes under the 1/4" green and 5/8" natural pieces and over the 3/8" piece.

Continue to weave to the right and left of the center piece, alternating 1/4" flat green and 5/8" natural. With all the pieces woven in place, measure and true the base to 6" x 13". As in **Diagram 2**, bend all the 3/8" filler pieces over toward the center of the base and tuck them under the second row of 5/8" flat.

Soak a long piece of #3 round reed until it is pliable, fold it almost in half, and begin twining as in **Diagram 3**. The "top" weaver always goes under the next stake in twining. Twine around the base one time. End the twining by tucking the ends under itself where it began. Upsett the stakes by bending each stake over on itself toward the base making a crease at the base of the stake. See **Diagram 4**.

UPSETTING THE SIDES & WEAVING
The sides are woven by the start-stop method. See **Dia-**

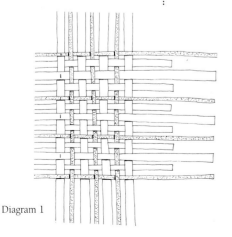

Diagram 1

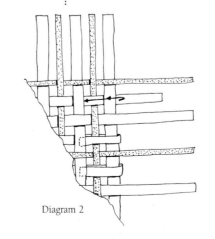

Diagram 2

gram 5 for how to begin and end a row. Start every row at a different place so as to avoid a build-up from the overlapping. Begin a long soaked piece of brown 5/8" on the outside of a green stake, weave around the basket moving over and under stakes, and end by going over the beginning of the weaver for 4 stakes. Cut so the end is hidden.

In the start-stop method, weave the following rows:

- 5 rows of 5/8" brown
- 2 rows of 1/4" green
- 4 rows of 5/8" natural

At this point, make the green "leaves," which are curls made from 3/8" flat green reed. Start a soaked piece of 3/8" flat behind a 5/8" stake on the top row of 5/8" natural flat reed. Place the smooth side of the leaf against the 5/8" weaver. Loop it around, making the smooth side stay on the outside, take it down to the first row of 5/8" and behind the 1/4" green stake. From there

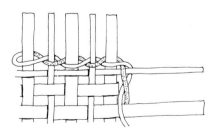

Diagram 3

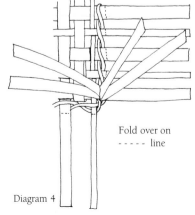

Fold over on
- - - - line

Diagram 4

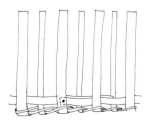

Diagram 5

loop again and take the piece back up to the first natural 5/8" flat row and under the 5/8" natural stake. See **Diagram 6**. Continue all the way around the basket, alternately going under the stakes. When the green leaves are done, weave 2 more start-stop rows with 1/2" flat (natural) reed. Now do 2 rows of "flowers," curls made from 1/4" dyed rose over the top (fourth) row of 5/8" natural and 1/2" flat rows. See **Diagram 6**. Weave 3 rows of 1/4" flat natural.

WEAVING GRADUATED SIDES

Soak a long piece of natural 1/4" reed. Taper one end for several inches. Looking at **Diagram 7**, place the end behind the fourth 5/8" flat stake on the end of the basket.

Weave to the opposite end in an over 1, under 1 weave, turn around stake 2 and weave back to the beginning. This time turn around stake 6. The weaver turns and reverses direction 1 stake short of the row before. See **Diagram 8** for a side view of the decreasing rows. End with the weaver going under and over 5 stakes. When one side is finished, begin a new soaked, tapered weaver on the other side and repeat the procedure.

INSERTING HANDLES & FINISHING STAKES

Numbering the stakes from left to right, insert the handles on both sides with the fourth and tenth stakes. Push handles behind only 1 or 2 weavers, making sure the notches fall just above

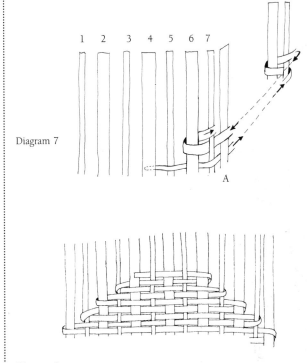

1 2 3 4 5 6 7

A

Diagram 7

Diagram 8

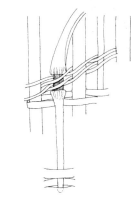

Diagram 9

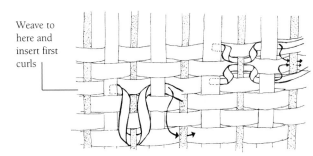

Weave to here and insert first curls

Diagram 6

115

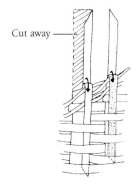

Cut away —

Diagram 10

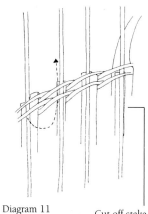

Diagram 11

Cut off stake in
front of handle

Diagram 12

the top row of weaving. See **Diagram 9**.

With a long soaked #3 round reed weaver, begin twining anywhere around the stakes just above the weaving. Fold the #3 round reed weaver and loop it around a stake. See previous instructions for how to twine. Twine 2 rows and end by tucking the end under the twined area where it began.

Point all the stakes and trim half the width away as in **Diagram 10**. Push the stakes behind a row or two of weaving on the inside of the basket. Cut the stakes

with which the handles are placed instead of turning them to the inside.

MAKING THE BORDER

Locate the 40 pieces of #4 round reed that were cut 36". They will be used to make the border. Soak all the pieces until they are pliable. Push one end of a piece of round reed under the twining on the outside of the basket extending about 1/3 of the reed above the twining. Place 1 piece on top of every stake around the basket. See **Diagram 11**.

Then, as in **Diagram 12**, move the lower portion of

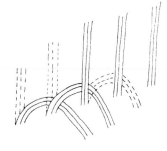

Diagram 13

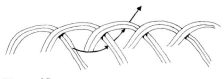

Diagram 15

the round reed up under the twining on the stake to the right, pulling both ends at the same time so they will be even at the top. Leave a "scallop" under the twining. See **Diagram 12**.

The 2 pieces on top of each stake are now treated as one.

STEP I: Bend each spoke to the right, behind the spoke to its right and to the outside. See **Diagram 13**. The last spoke goes behind the first one that is already in place. See **Diagram 14**.

STEP II: Starting anwhere, move each spoke over the one to its right and to the inside of the basket. See **Diagram 15**. Again, the last stake must go over the first stake that is already in place. At the end of the 2 step procedure, the rim should resemble **Diagram 16**.

Working from the inside of the basket now, repeat the last 2 steps, taking each spoke under the one to its right and up. See **Diagram 17**. Then, as before, take each spoke over the one to its right and down beside the wall of the basket. See **Diagram 18**. Should you need additional help with this border, see the "Up Close" section.

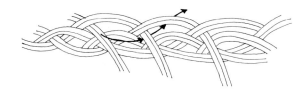

Diagram 16

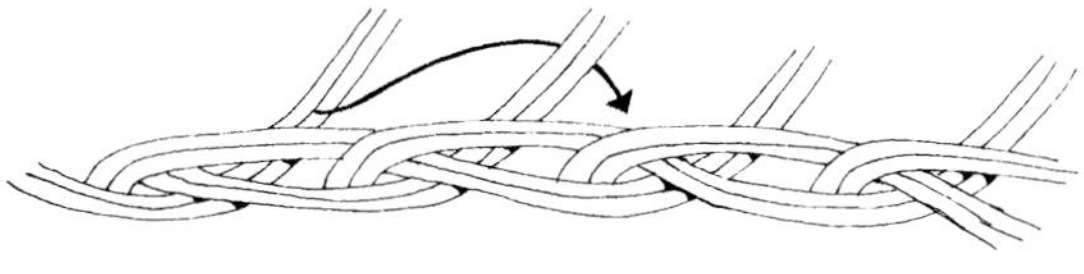

Diagram 17

Diagram 18

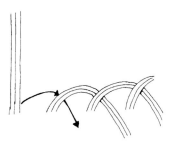

Diagram 14

Provender Basket

Probably few baskets evoke images of the English country-side and gathering fresh flowers as readily as this one does. It is made here from flat reed spokes and round reed weavers dyed the color of your choice. The lacy border only adds to its Victorian image. Thanks to Dianne Craver of Candler, North Carolina, for helping with the creation of this basket.

APPROXIMATE SIZE
18" x 15" x 12" high

MATERIALS
5/8" flat reed (spokes)
#3 round reed (weavers)
Handle 31" long (23" notch to notch) with 14" to 15" span

PRELIMINARY STEP

Dye approximately 1/2 hank of #3 round reed the color of your choice, following the directions on the dye package. To insure colorfast dying, have the water just before boiling when the reed is immersed.

WEAVING THE BASKET

From the 5/8" flat reed, cut 10 pieces 24" long. Mark the centers of all the pieces on the wrong (rough) side. Soak all the pieces until they are pliable. Lay them as in **Diagram 1**, making sure spokes 1 and 2 are perpendicular to each other.

Soak a long piece of the dyed #3 round reed until it is pliable. Fold it almost in half and begin twining as in **Diagram 2**, placing the fold around a spoke. The top weaver always goes under the next spoke in twining. Twine for 4 rows. Stop twining and end the weavers, as in **Diagram 3**, on the outside of the base.

With scissors, cut every spoke but 1 into 3 equal parts (lengthwise), stopping just before the twining. Cut the odd spoke in half. This will result in having 59 spokes. *Note:* The total number of spokes is important because the basket will be woven in an over 3, under 2 twill in a continuous weave. The total must be a number divisible by 5 (the total number in the stroke), plus or minus 1. Fifty-nine is, of course, 60 (divisible by 5) minus 1.

Turn the base over so the right side is up. Soak a long piece of dyed #3 round reed and begin again, as in **Diagram 4**, by pushing it between any 2 spokes. The weaver moves over 3 spokes and under 2 spokes and because of its total number, steps over 1 spoke when the weaving returns to the starting point creating a spiral design. Much packing is required, as the weaving will have a tendency to slip out toward the edges of the spokes. Pack each row firmly against the row before. Also, make every effort to make the base lie flat on the table. The edges will also have a tendency to curl. Weave until the diameter is approximately 17". Add new weavers as needed, as in **Diagram 5**, by laying the new weaver in beside the old one on the back (outside) of the basket.

When the diameter is as large as you want it, stop the weaver by tucking it into the woven area. Begin another long soaked piece of dyed #3 round reed by folding it

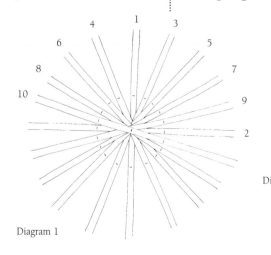

Diagram 1

Diagram 2

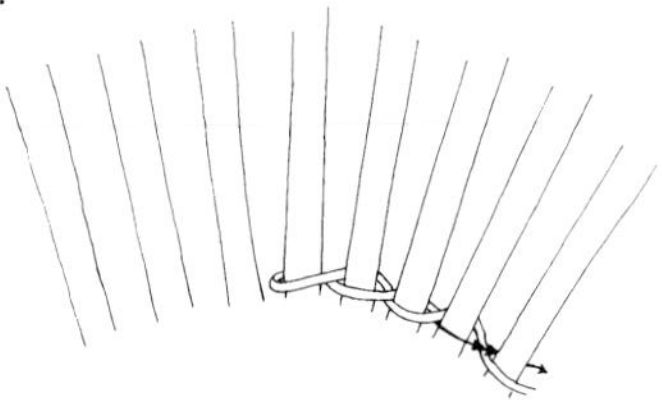

Diagram 3

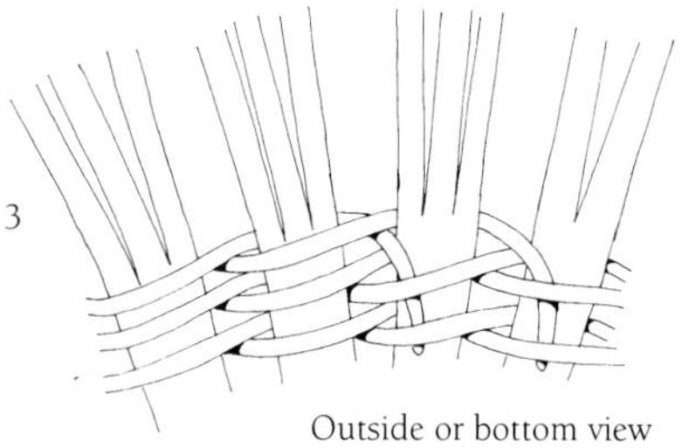

Outside or bottom view

almost in half and looping the fold around a spoke. Twine with both ends of the weavers for 4 rows. See **Diagram 6**. Stop both the weavers by pushing the ends into the twined area beside 2 consecutive spokes as before.

FINISHING THE SPOKES & MAKING THE BORDER

Rewet the ends of the spokes if they have dried. Point all the ends of the spokes, as in **Diagram 7**, and bend them over the twined area to the outside of the basket, pushing them behind several rows of weaving.

From the dyed #3 round reed, cut 29 pieces 36" long. Soak them until they are pliable. Insert the handle into the weaving with any 2 spokes that are directly opposite each other, letting the notch fall just below the twining. See **Diagram 8**.

Insert each of the 29 pieces of round reed by

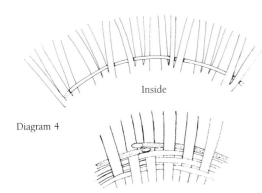

Inside

Diagram 4

Diagram 5

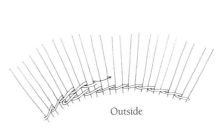

Outside

Diagram 6

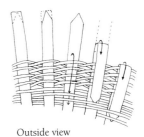

Outside view

Diagram 7

Diagram 8

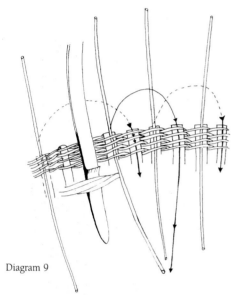

Diagram 9

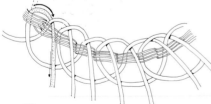

Diagram 10

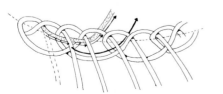

Diagram 11

pushing one end into the weaving on top of a spoke *toward the center of the basket*. Push the other end into the weaving with the third spoke to the right, and pull both ends at the same time, leaving a 1" deep scallop on the outside of the basket and making the ends even. All the pieces are inserted in this manner except the last one, which must go into the weaving with the fourth spoke. If you begin the insertions at the handle and work around the basket, the last one to be inserted will also be at the handle, which is the least noticeable spot. See **Diagram 9**.

Holding the basket so the border pieces are pointing away from you, and starting anywhere, take each spoke behind the spoke to its right and to the outside. See **Diagram 10**. The last spoke is shaded in **Diagram 10** and must be pushed behind the first spoke that is already in place.

Holding the basket so the spokes are pointing toward you, again starting anywhere,

take each spoke over the next 2 spokes to the right (under the 2 ends) and to the inside (toward the center of the base). In **Diagram 11**, the arrow on the right shows the path of the first spoke; the left arrow shows the path of the last spoke, which must be pushed over the first 2 spokes that are already in place.

The next movement does nothing except move the spokes from the inside of the basket to the outside. Going over the 2 spokes to the right, take each spoke to the outside under the border that is woven in place. See **Diagram 12**.

Working with the spokes toward you, take each one over the one to its right and down. This simple rolled border can be repeated as many times as you want each time ending the last spoke by going over the first spoke that is already in place. See **Diagram 13**. Make as many rows as needed to cover the edge of the basket and stop just before the scalloped border.

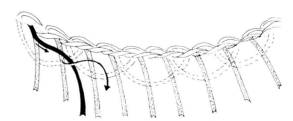

Diagram 12

Diagram 13

ECLECTIC

Round Reed Wall Basket

This attractive and usable wall pouch was designed by Dianne Stanton of Pembroke, Massachusetts. Your imagination is your only limitation as to how and where it could be used in your home. The seashell can be replaced by any number of items to fit your particular decorating theme.

APPROXIMATE SIZE
6" wide x 10" high

MATERIALS
#5 round reed (spokes)
#3 round reed (weavers)
#2 round reed (weavers)

PRELIMINARY STEP

Dye 6 to 8 long pieces of #3 round reed the color of your choice. The center section can be done with 1 color or 2, as in the example.

MAKING THE BASKET

From the natural #5 round reed, cut 8 pieces 32" long and 1 piece 16" long.

Mark the centers of the 8 pieces. Hold them together in groups of 4 with clothespins. As in **Diagram 1**, lay one group of 4 spokes over and perpendicular to the other group of 4. Align center marks.

Soak a long natural #2 round reed (weaver) and begin weaving around the 4 groups as in **Diagram 2**, by weaving over a top group and under the next (bottom) group, over the other top group and under the next bottom group for 3 rows. Push the "tail" of the beginning weaver discreetly between 2 spokes to be cut later.

Note: You will be weaving in a clockwise direction if you are right-handed and counterclockwise if you are left-handed.

After weaving 3 rounds, separate the groups into pairs of 2, and weave over 2, under 2 through 3 of the original groups. When you reach the 4th group, locate the 16" piece you cut. Cut one end at an angle, make a space with an awl between the first and second spokes of that 4th group and insert the 16" pointed spoke as far as possible into the weaving. See **Diagram 3**. Now weave through the 4th group over 2 (the new spoke and one of the original ones), under 2, and over 1. This single spoke will remain alone while the rest will be in pairs.

Weave around the second row. Now the weave will be opposite from the first row. See **Diagram 4**. You must start to shape very early with this basket. After the second row of weaving, pinch the base and force the spokes into a cone shape, holding the base and pointing the spokes away from you.

The "front" of the basket will have 4 original spokes and the "back" will have the group of 5 (4 original plus the added 1). All the time you are weaving the basket, make a concerted effort to keep the back of the basket flat and the spokes straight.

Continue to weave around in pairs for 8 rows. *Remember:* You will see 4 rows on top and 4 under to make a total of 8 rows.

When you arrive at the "single spoke" on the 8th row, separate all the pairs into singles thereafter. See **Diagram 5**. You will weave over and under single spokes for the rest of the basket.

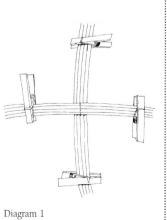

Diagram 1

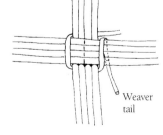

Weaver tail

Diagram 2

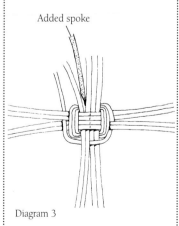

Added spoke

Diagram 3

To add a weaver, leave the end of the old one on the inside of the basket. Lay the end of a new one behind the same spoke as the old one, overlapping the ends for approximately 1", and without applying too much pressure, continue weaving with the new one. See **Diagram 6**.

When there is approximately 1/2" between spokes, you may want to change to #3 round reed for the weaving material.

When you have woven approximately 4" (front measurement), change to the color of your choice. See **Diagram 7**.

Some "turnbacks" must be done to make the back of the basket higher than the front. As you are weaving "over 1-under 1" anytime after about 4" of weaving, you must do several rows of turnbacks—that is, turn around a spoke and reverse directions. The first turnback should be made around the left-hand spoke in the mid-

Added spoke

Diagram 4

Diagram 5

Diagram 6

Diagram 7

3" - 4"

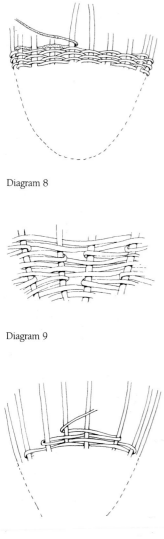

Diagram 8

Diagram 9

Diagram 10

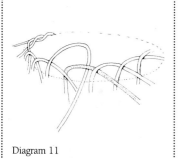

Diagram 11

dle of the front. See **Diagram 8**. Weave around the basket to the middle right-hand spoke on the front. Turn back around that spoke and reverse directions again. As in **Diagram 9**, continue to reverse directions by dropping back 1 spoke each turn, until you are weaving around only the middle 3 spokes on the back. See **Diagram 10**.

Weave all the way around the basket 2 times (without turning back). Repeat the "turning back" rows.

Note: All the packing or turning back is done in colored reed.

After the colored turning-back rows are done twice, finish weaving the basket in natural reed. There should be 7 rows of natural #3

Diagram 12

Diagram 13

round reed woven after the color, and the spokes should be about 6" long. These ends will be used to make the border. End the weaver by pushing it down into the weaving beside a spoke.

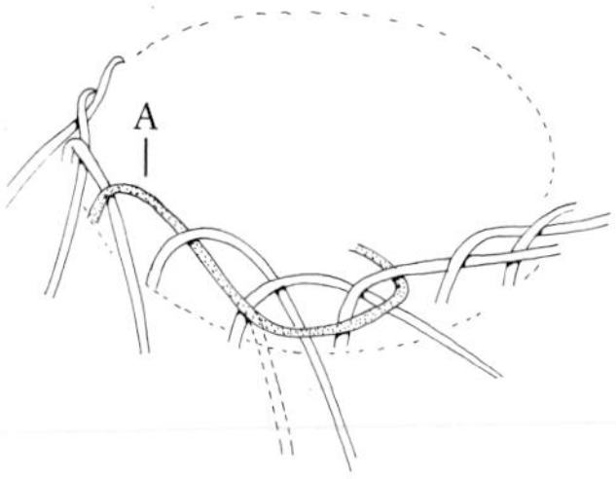

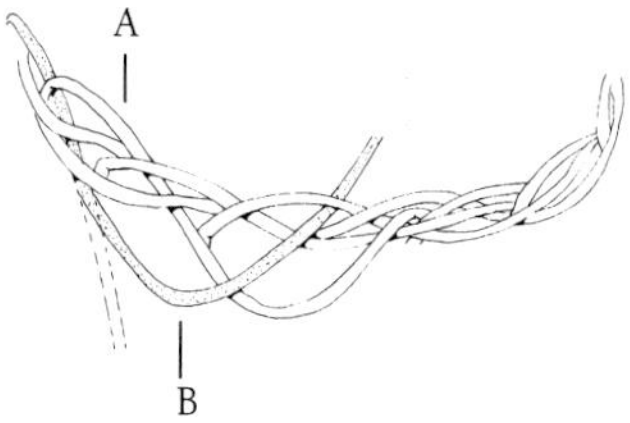

MAKING THE BORDER

Resoak the ends of the spokes if they have dried. Bend each spoke to the right behind the spoke to its right and bring it to the outside. The last spoke must go behind the first one that is already bent in place. See **Diagram 11**.

Next, starting anywhere, take each spoke over the 2 spokes to its right and to the inside. See **Diagram 12**. The last spoke must also go over 2 and to the inside. See **Diagram 13**. Trim the ends so

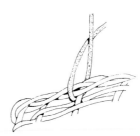

Diagram 14

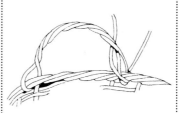

Diagram 15

they lie flat against a spoke on the inside.

MAKING THE HANDLE

Soak a piece of #3 round reed that is about 28" long. Loop it in half under the border on the left side of the back. See **Diagram 14**.

Twist the 2 pieces together as in **Diagram 15**, then take the 2 ends under the border on the right side of the back. Twist the rest of the reed around the handle already in place and tuck the ends either in the first loop or under the border.

Attach the seashell or other decorative item to the front as in **Diagrams 16 & 17**, tying the ends of the reed that threaded through the shell inside.

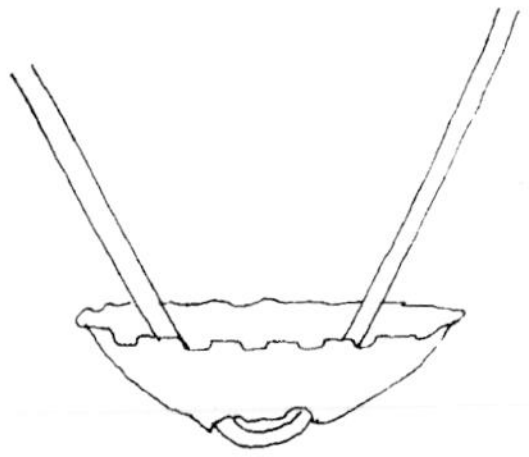

Diagram 16

Diagram 17

This extraordinary basket was designed by Sosse Baker of Chester, Connecticut. Sosse's shaping technique is wonderfully simple (at least when she does it!), requiring only some practice. The total number of stakes must be a number divisible by 7 plus 4. The basket described here has a total of 32 stakes (28, which is divisible by 7, plus 4 = 32). Try other sizes on your own.

APPROXIMATE SIZE OVERALL
9" Diameter x 13" High

MATERIALS
1/4" flat or flat oval or
    7mm flat oval reed (stakes)
11/64" flat oval reed
    (weavers)
1/2" half round (rim)
#15 round reed (handle)
    or a purchased handle

One-Two-Three Twill

PRELIMINARY STEP

To form the handle, soak a piece of #15 round reed for an hour (or until it bends easily). Choose the shape you want your handle to take. Locate or construct a form—pegs driven into a board or a round or square hoop. The example here uses a square hoop. Make a center mark on the reed. Next, mark 1" and 2" to the right and left of the center mark. Mark a center on the hoop. Aligning the center marks, bend the round reed around the hoop and hold in place with heavy-duty clamps until it dries. Remove when dry. With a knife or trimming plane and sand paper, carve the handle on the marks and sand until smooth. Notch the handles approximately 3" from the ends, cutting through half the thickness of the reed at the notch and tapering the thickness until it becomes very thin at the end. See **Diagrams A-E** on page 128.

From the 1/4" flat reed (or whatever material you are using for stakes), cut 32 pieces 28" long. Dye them the color of your choice. Mark the centers on the smooth side and soak them until they are pliable.

MAKING THE BASE

Lay 16 pieces of stake material horizontally, aligning center marks, right (smooth) side up. Weave one of the other 16 pieces vertically just to the right of the center marks as in **Diagram 1**, going under 2, over 2, etc., ending with over 2.

Looking at **Diagram 2**, weave 6 more pieces to the right and 8 pieces to the left of the center mark in a 2/2 twill. All these are woven right side up. Measure and true the base to approximately 4-3/4" x 4-3/4".

WEAVING THE SIDES

Soak a long piece of 11/64" flat oval reed. Begin weaving as in **Diagram 3**, with the end going over 2, under 2. Weave with the base on a flat surface for several rows. As you weave keep the right side of the weaver up. Do not allow it to turn at the corners. Weave the first row of over 2, under 2 as closely and snugly as possible.

With one revolution of over 2, under 2 complete, begin the pattern weave as in **Diagram 4** * weaving over 3, under 1, over 1, under 2, repeating from * all the way up the sides of the basket. The weave is continuous, not one row at a time.

From the very first row, spread the stakes from the center stake outward toward the corners. By the fourth or fifth row, the corners should be completely filled in with spokes as in **Diagram 4**. You

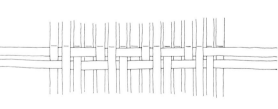

Diagram 1

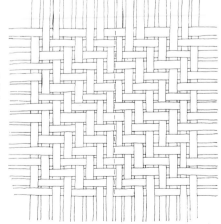

Diagram 2

must hold the spokes in place with one hand and weave with the other as you round the corners. Use clothespins if necessary. The pieces will stay in place after several rows of forced placing. After the fifth row, as in **Diagram 5**, lift the base, place your thumbs on the inside of the basket and press down on the corners, bending the sides of the basket. You are creating the "cat-head" shape on the bottom of the basket. **Diagram 6** shows the basic shape for which you are aiming. Replace the basket on a flat surface and continue weaving for 2 or 3 more rows, repeating the shaping procedure as needed.

Note: Everyone must find his or her own shaping method. You may find you want to lift the basket sooner. Experiment to see what works best for you.

Lift the base, holding it with ends of stakes pointed away from you, and continue weaving around the basket. The sides will begin to stand up. You must control and create the shape you want.

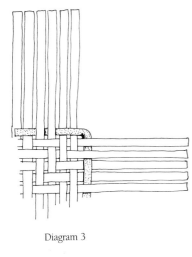

Diagram 3

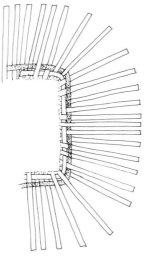

Diagram 4

Diagram 5

The longer the base remains on a flat surface, the fuller the sides will be. The sooner it is held with stakes pointing away from you, the straighter the sides will be.

Ideally, the shape should resemble **Diagram 7**, with a diameter of approximately 10" at the fullest point and approximately 8" or 9" at the neck. Naturally, to bring the sides in, increase the tension on the weaver and press inward on the stakes, being careful not to tighten too quickly.

FINISHING THE BASKET
When the weaving is within 2-1/2" of the ends of the stakes, taper the weaver for several inches, making it 1/8"

at its narrowest. Cut the stakes on the inside of the basket flush with the top row. Rewet and point the remaining stakes; bend them over the top row and tuck them under the first available row of weaving on the inside of the basket. See **Diagram 8** for a detail of the pointed and tucked stake. Insert the handle as in **Diagram 9** on the outside of the basket, pushing the ends only under 2 or 3 rows of weaving so the notch falls on the top row. Cut 2 pieces of 1/2" half round reed, each long enough to reach around the top of the basket and overlap at least 2".

Place the rim pieces around the top of the basket, covering 2 rows of weaving.

Mark in pencil on both ends where the ends overlap. Remove from basket. With a knife or trimming plane, bevel the area of overlap from both ends so the overlapped area is no thicker than a single thickness of 1/2" half round.

Replace the rim on the basket, placing the overlapped areas near, but not on top of, each other. Hold it in place with clothespins. See **Diagram 10**. Soak a long piece of natural 3/16" flat oval until it is pliable. Lash the rim pieces in place, "hooking" the end over the basket wall just past the overlapped areas, as in **Diagram 10**. The lasher goes under the inside rim, over

the wall and behind a weaver on the outside of the basket. With the long end, lash around the rim, going in every space between stakes. "X" the handle if you wish as in **Diagram 11**. The lasher is moving from outside to inside around the rim. When the handle is reached (5) the X is made by going diagonally to 6, up behind the rim to 7, diagonally across to 8, up behind the rim on the left of the handle to 9, and over the first stroke of the X from 9 to 10, where regular lashing resumes. Repeat on the other side of the handle.

End lashing as it began, or tuck the end discreetly under a weaver on the inside of the basket.

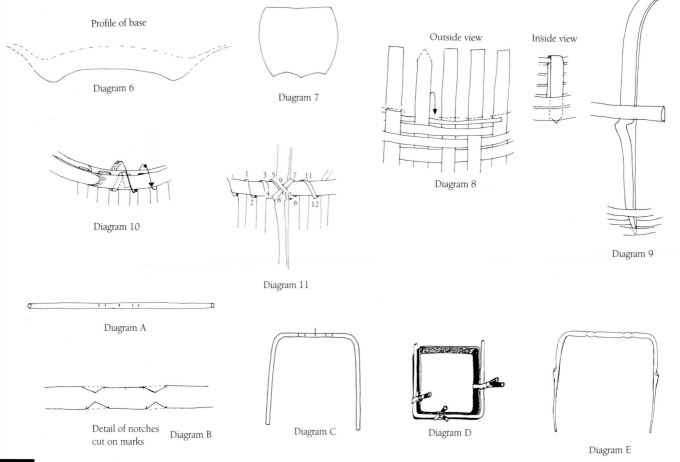

Profile of base

Diagram 6

Diagram 7

Outside view   Inside view

Diagram 8

Diagram 10

Diagram 9

Diagram 11

Diagram A

Detail of notches cut on marks   Diagram B

Diagram C

Diagram D

Diagram E

Diagonal Blocks

I learned the weaving techniques used in this basket from my multitalented friend Theresa Ohno of Seattle, Washington. The lovely base is most unusual. When it isn't in use, hang it so the base shows. It can be made in any color combination, but I have used 3 shades of one color, directions for which are given.

APPROXIMATE SIZE
8" diameter x 4-1/2" high

MATERIALS
#4 round reed (spokes)
#3 round reed (weavers)
Dye (your choice)

PRELIMINARY STEP

Using only 3 or 4 strands of the #3 round reed per bundle, roll several bundles into coils that will fit your dye pot.

Fill an enamel pot with half the amount of water specified on the dye package. This will make a strong, concentrated dye and should be your darkest shade. Dye test pieces of reed each time you change shades before you immerse the coils.

When the dye is just before boiling, dip the coils in, one at a time, until they are the shade you want. The longer they stay in, the darker they become.

You will need twice as much of the darkest shade of reed as of the other 2 shades.

When you have dyed all the reed you want in the darkest shade, add at least the same amount of water with which you began, diluting the dye to half the original strength. Repeat the dying process with more coils of reed for the medium shade.

For the lightest shade, add as much water as you need to obtain the shade desired. It may be necessary to remove some of the dye before adding more water.

WEAVING THE BASE

Cut 16 pieces of #4 round reed 34" long. Mark the centers on all the pieces and 2" on each side of the centers. The 2" marks will form a guideline on which you should begin weaving the original circle. Lay the 16 pieces, as in **Diagram 1**, in groups of 4. Note the placement of the center marks on **Diagram 1**. On each of the 4 sides, there will be 2 groups with 4 spokes in each group. Mentally number the 4 spokes in each group 1 to 4 according to the diagram.

Soak a long piece of #3 round reed until it is pliable. Fold it almost in half. Pinch the fold with needle nose pliers. Place the fold around the number 1 spokes from each of the 2 groups in any one of the sections. Twine around the spokes 2 at a time, the "1s" together, the "2s" together, "3s" together and the "4s" together. Go on to the next group until you have twined all the way around the center circle. See **Diagram 2**. Twine continuously (one row after another) for 6 rows. Should you need to add a weaver, do so as in **Diagram 3**, stopping the old one at one spoke and adding the new one at the spoke before. After 6 rows, split the pairs of spokes into single spokes and continue to twine around the base for 4 more rows or until the diameter of the base is approximately 8". End both weavers by pushing

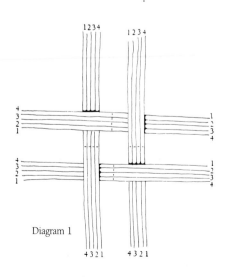

Diagram 1

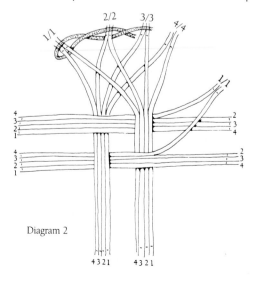

Diagram 2

the ends into the twined area beside 2 consecutive spokes. See **Diagram 4**.

Resoak the spokes at the base if they have dried and while doing a row of 4-rod wale, upsett them.

Soak 4 long pieces of #3 round reed dyed the darkest shade.

Begin as in **Diagram 5** by placing the ends of each of the 4 pieces behind 4 consecutive spokes. Mentally or otherwise, number these 4 spokes 1, 2, 3 and 4. It is a good idea to place a twist tie or string around spoke 1 as a marker. Lifting the farthest left weaver each stroke, take it over the 3 spokes to the right, behind the fourth and to the outside. Each weaver continues this pattern in turn. Upon returning to the starting spokes, stop the weaver behind the same spokes where they began. Do not cut the weavers. See **Diagram 6**.

WEAVING THE SIDES

The weaving technique used on the sides is a chase weave done with sets of weavers. As in a regular weave-chase,

one weaver (set) is used until it catches the previous one. Then another set is used, again until it catches the one before it.

Soak several long weavers of each of the 3 shades.

Behind spokes 5, 6 and 7, start respectively a light, medium and dark weaver. These 3 weavers make up the first set, which in **Diagrams 6, 7, 8** and **9** is shaded with dots. Even though the set consists of 3 different shades, the shading designates a set. The next set is shaded with lines and the third set is shaded solid black. Work 1 row of 3-rod wale, as in **Diagram 7**, always lifting the farthest left weaver and taking it over the 2 spokes to the right behind the third and back to the outside. **Diagram 8** illustrates that the first set of weavers stops behind the 3 spokes immediately before 1, 2, 3 and 4.

Start 3 more weavers in the same order as the weavers in set 1 (light, medium and dark) behind spokes 8, 9 and 10, and work a 3-rod wale around the basket,

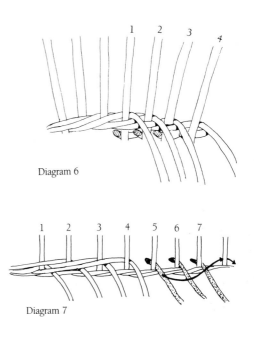

Diagram 6

Diagram 7

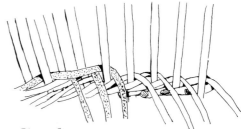

Diagram 8

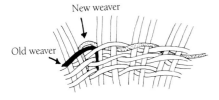

Diagram 3

Diagram 4

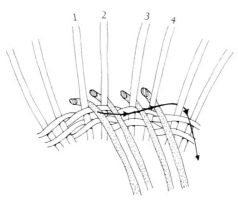

Diagram 5

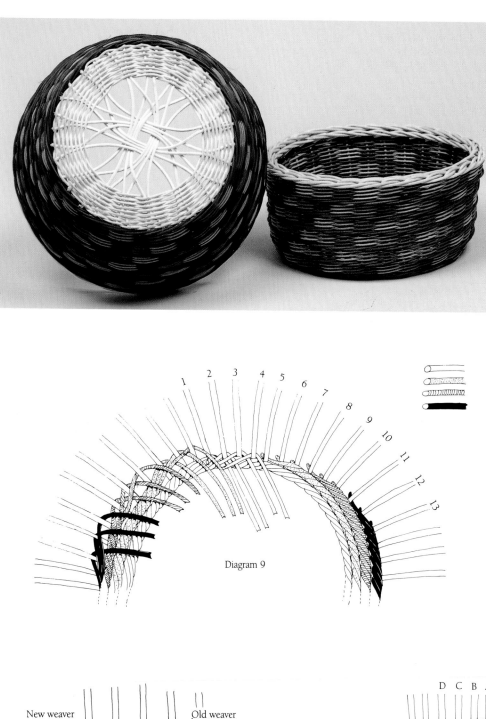

stopping again behind the 3 spokes immediately before the end of set 1.

Again, start 3 new weavers in the same order as before—light, medium and dark—and repeat the 3-rod wale to the spokes immediately before the second set. In **Diagram 9**, you can see where all weavers start and stop on the first row around.

With the third set of 3 weavers woven around as far as it can go, return to the first 4 weavers and work 4-rod wale until they are immediately before the last set of 3. Drop the 4 weavers and pick up set 1 weavers and work 3-rod wale until it catches up with the 4 weavers. Continue this process, dropping one set when it catches the previous set. Don't forget that 3 sets make a 3-rod wale and the other set is 4-rod wale. Should you need to add on a weaver, do so as in **Diagram 10** by either tucking the old weaver into the weaving

1 2 3 4 5 6 7 8 9 10 11 12 13

Diagram 9

New weaver   Old weaver

Diagram 10

Inside view
Adding new weaver

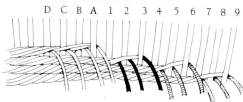

D C B A 1 2 3 4 5 6 7 8 9

Diagram 11

beside a spoke or letting it lie on the inside of the spoke. Push the end of the new weaver into the weaving beside the previous spoke.

Weave in this manner, one set at a time, until there are 6 rows of blocks.

On the final row, stop the first set of 3 weavers when they are behind spokes 7, 8 and 9, which were the last 3 spokes behind which weavers were started. The second set of weavers should end behind spokes 6, 5 and 4, and the third behind 3, 2 and 1. See **Diagram 11**. The set of 4 will continue to weave above the weavers that have ended to end behind spokes 10, 11, 12 and 13. See **Diagram 12**. Cut the weavers 1" to 2" long and leave them to dry on the inside of the basket. They should be trimmed to 1/2" later.

MAKING THE BORDER

Soak all the ends of the spokes thoroughly so they won't break when they bend. Now bend any 1 to the right, behind the spoke to its right and back to the outside. See **Diagram 13**. The last spoke must be pushed behind the first spoke that was bent to the right and is already in place. Lift it enough for the last spoke to go behind it. End as in **Diagram 14**.

Starting anywhere, take each spoke over the 2 spokes to its right and to the inside of the basket. See **Diagram 15**. The last spoke must go over the first 2 that are already in place. See **Diagram 16**. Once all the spokes are on the inside, make a rolled border on the inside. Take any one over the 2 spokes to its right and down beside the wall of the basket. Repeat the process as many times around as you want. See **Diagram 17**. As with the other border, the last spoke must be pushed over the first 2 spokes and down to the inside.

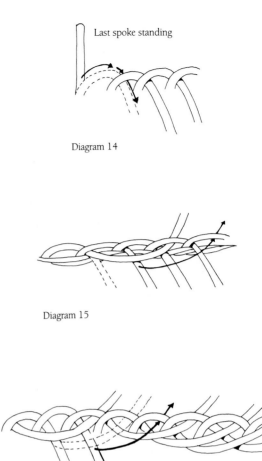

Last spoke standing

Diagram 14

Diagram 15

Last 2 spokes

Diagram 16

Diagram 17

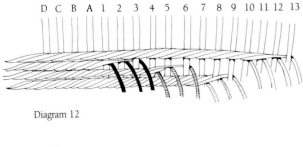

D C B A 1 2 3 4 5 6 7 8 9 10 11 12 13

Diagram 12

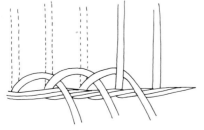

Diagram 13

Undulating Twill

Thanks to Judith Olney of Rowley, Massachusetts, for sharing her ideas and techniques for making this twill weave basket. Some weaving suggestions are given, but don't be afraid to experiment with your own ideas. The weave is always interesting, however it is done. Shaping is entirely under your control.

APPROXIMATE SIZE

12" diameter x 12" high

MATERIALS

1/4" flat reed (stakes)
3/16" flat oval reed cut in half lengthwise (weavers)
11/64" flat oval reed (weavers)
1/4" or 7mm flat oval reed (weavers)
1/2" half round reed (rim)
11/64" flat or common cane, used reed side out (lashing)

PRELIMINARY STEP

Dye the weavers the color of your choice. Before dying, all the wider pieces should be tapered down to the width of 3/16" cut in half.

The weaving pattern on the sides of the basket is a continuous weave of over 3, under 2. You can make any size basket you want, but consider that the total number of stakes must be divisible by 5 plus 1 or plus 4. For example, making a square base that is 16 stakes by 16 stakes gives a total number of 64 which is divisible by 5 (plus 4). Another manageable size to consider is a 19 x 19: 76 total, which is divisible by 5 (75 plus 1).

The stakes must stay relatively close together (1/4") so the weaving pattern is provided a background.

From the 1/4" flat reed, cut 32 pieces 32" long. Mark the centers of all the pieces on the wrong side. Soak all the pieces until they are pliable.

WEAVING THE BASE

The base is a 2/2 (over 2, under 2) twill. As in **Diagram 1**, lay 4 stakes horizontally with the centers aligned. Either mentally or actually, number them 1 to 4 with number 1 closest to you. Placing the center marks above the #4 horizontal stake, weave the next 4 stakes vertically, to the right of the center marks on the horizontal pieces in the following pattern:

1. under 1 and 2, over 3 and 4
2. under 2 and 3, over 1 and 4
3. under 3 and 4, over 1 and 2
4. under 1 and 4, over 2 and 3

Diagram 2 shows the first 4 rows of pattern woven to the right of the center marks.

Repeat the pattern until half the vertical stakes are in place to the right of the center marks. **Diagram 2** also shows 2 stakes woven to the left of the center marks. Row 1 on the left is a repeat of row 4 on the right, and row 2 is a repeat of row 3, etc. The stakes to the left are simply in a reverse pattern of the ones to the right. Finished, there should be 8 pieces to the right of the center and 8 to the left.

Now, weave the remaining horizontal pieces, 4 more below the center marks and 8 above. If you still have problems with the twill pattern, turn the base 1/4 turn. Repeat the weaving pattern of the 4 now vertical stakes (1-4) to the right and reversed (4-1) to the left. **Diagram 3** shows the finished base.

FRAMING THE BASE

The first row of weaving is a start-stop row using an 11/64" or 3/16" flat reed

Diagram 1

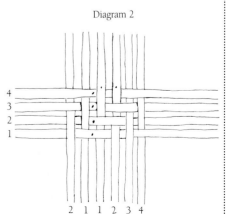

Diagram 2

cut in half. The important thing about this row is that the weaver must move from outside to inside or inside to outside at the corners. The weaving pattern on this row only is over 2, under 2. The rest of the basket is over 3, under 2. Try starting at several different places, anticipating the corners. If 2/2 doesn't work, go over 1, under 1 or over 2, under 1 at the corners—whatever you have to do to make the transition from outside to inside or vise versa at the corners. See **Diagram 4**. Do not allow the weaver to flip over at the corner. Rather, make it go about 1/8" beyond the edge of the last stake and bend the weaver back on itself, making a crease before turning the corner. See **Diagram 5** for ending the first row.

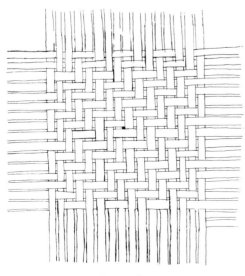

Diagram 3

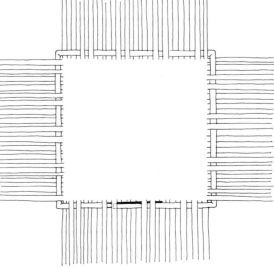

Diagram 4

Diagram 5

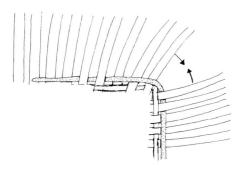

Diagram 6

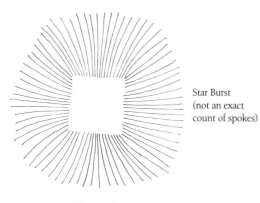

Star Burst
(not an exact
count of spokes)

Diagram 7

WEAVING THE SIDES

Turn the base over so the right side is up. You are now weaving on the outside of the basket and will continue to for the entire basket. Begin with 11/64" flat oval reed that has been tapered, starting on the side opposite you. Weave over 3, under 2, etc., the rest of the basket. As you weave, work the stakes toward the corner in order to fill the corners and achieve a sunburst of stakes. See **Diagram 6**. All the corners should be filled by the sixth row around. See **Diagram 7**.

Leave the base lying flat as you weave around for at least 8 rows. After the 8 rows, lift the basket and hold it with the stakes pointing away from you and continue to weave from the outside. The sides will begin to go up immediately almost on their own, so be careful they don't go up too fast.

As you weave around the basket, the over 3 moves over 1 stake each row, making the pattern spiral up the basket sides. When you need to add a weaver, change to a different width (with the end tapered to match the size you were using). Add

another piece, as in **Diagram 8**, starting the new one behind a stake before the old one runs out. Weave with both of them for several stakes and continue with the new one, ending the old one behind a stake. Consult the pattern options below to decide which widths to use and in what order.

REVERSING THE PATTERN

To reverse the weaving direction, you must make an intentional "mistake" in the same place in each row which will cause the weaving pattern to shift visually, but you will continue to weave in the same direction. For instance, if you are weaving right-handed (to the right around the basket) and the weaving pattern is moving to the right, when you make the mistake, you will continue to weave right-handed around the basket, but the weaving pattern will begin to move to the left. On a 16 x 16 stake basket, the mistake is "over 2, under 1." When you have woven as far as you want in one direction, and you have enough weaver remaining to go around the basket 2 times, taper the weaver so it is almost thread-

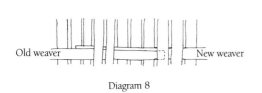

Old weaver   New weaver

Diagram 8

Diagram 9

like. Near the end of the second round, make the mistake which will reverse the pattern. Add a new weaver that is tapered just as thin as the other one was for at least 2 more rows. This way the "point" of the pattern, formed when it reversed, looks more defined because of the very skinny weaver. **Diagram 9** illustrates the weaving pattern moving to the right, then the mistake row and 2 more rows with the pattern reversed, showing the mistake still being made. Notice that the mistake is technically in the same place every row, but the "same place" moves over 1 stake every row. If you have trouble knowing when to make the mistake, put a string or twist tie around the first stake in the over 2 the first time you do it and move it 1 stake every row to help you spot the place to make the mistake.

Note: On a 19 x 19 stake basket the mistake is either over 4, under 3 or under 4, over 3. Use whichever works for you.

Weave, making the mistake with the pattern reversed as far as you want. When you want to make the

pattern reverse to the right again, do not make the mistake any more. Simply return to the regular over 3, under 2 pattern instead of making the mistake.

The shape of the basket should resemble **Diagram 10**. You may reverse as many times as you want, but the undulation shows more clearly with larger areas moving in one direction. The undulation is achieved by changing from a wide weaver (7mm perhaps) to a very thin one (11/64" cut in half) for several rows. See **Diagram 11**. Remember to taper the wider weaver to the size of the smaller one when changing widths.

If you want the neck of the basket to decrease in diameter as the example does, push in on the stakes when you want to decrease and apply a little extra tension on the weaver.

When you are within 2" of the ends of the stakes, taper the weaver the width it was when you began weaving and stop directly above the starting place. See **Diagram 12**.

RIMMING THE BASKET
Soak a piece of 1/2" half

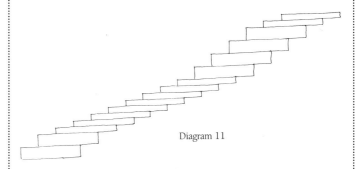

Diagram 11

Inside View

Diagram 12

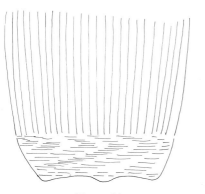

Diagram 10

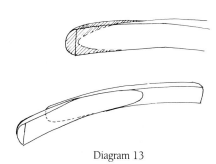

Diagram 13

Outside view

Outside view

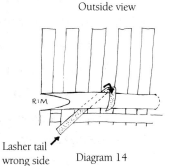

RIM

Lasher tail
wrong side

Diagram 14

Diagram 15

Inside view

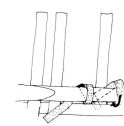

Diagram 16

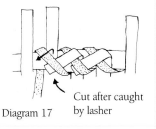

Diagram 17

Cut after caught
by lasher

Outside view

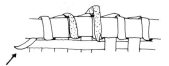

Lasher tail

Diagram 18

round reed that is long enough to reach around the rim once and overlap 2" to 3". Place it on the basket and mark the area of overlap. Remove it from the basket and, with a knife or plane, shave half the thickness from the top of one piece and half from the bottom of the other, so when they are overlapped, the thickness will be equal to that of a single thickness of half round reed. See **Diagram 13**. Dampen the ends of the stakes and a lasher. Taper one end of the lasher for about 6" and, as in **Diagram 14**, place the lasher behind a stake (the wrong side of the stake and the lasher should touch). Leave about 1" of lasher sticking out to the left, and angle the lasher from lower left to upper right behind the stake. The lasher comes to the outside of the basket between the stake it is behind and the next stake on the right. Place the rim piece against the outside of the stakes just at the top of the weaving. The beveled end of the rim should be placed just to the left of the stake that has the lasher behind it. **Diagram 14** shows the basket properly set up for lashing.

As in **Diagram 15**, take the lasher over the top of the rim, around and under the bottom, back to the inside of the basket through the same space between stakes. Pull down on the lasher inside the basket to seat the rim

firmly at the top of the weaving. Bend the stake the lasher went behind down to the right over against the inside of the basket. Bring the lasher up to the next right space between stakes, catching the bent stake as you do so. **Diagram 16** shows the steps you have just completed. After the stake has been folded over and caught by the lasher, it can be cut. **Diagram 17** shows 2 wraps around the rim and the third in progress.

Continue this process until you reach the start. The folded over stakes should lie flat against the inside of the basket. Pull very hard on the lasher. It should bind the bent over stakes to the rim as tightly as possible. At the point where the ends of the rim must overlap, you will have only 1 stake left standing, thin about 6" of the lasher nearest the basket to prevent lumps as the end of the lashing overlaps the beginning. Pull on the starting end to tighten the beginning of the lashing. Trace the beginning of the lashing, duplicating each wrap exactly. You will have to raise the bent over stakes to feed the end of the lashing under them. **Diagram 18** shows the ending of the weaving.

After you have duplicated 3 or 4 wraps around the rim, cut the lasher as it emerges from under a folded over stake. Trim the beginning of the lasher.

Melon Basket

PRELIMINARY STEP

From the #6 round reed, cut the following pieces:

- Primary ribs: 6 pieces 13-1/2" long
- Secondary ribs: 4 pieces 12" long

Keep primary and secondary ribs separate. Soak all the pieces for about 15 minutes or until they are pliable. Remove them from water and clip them around the 8" hoops as in **Diagram A**. Allow them to dry in place before beginning to make the basket.

PREPARING HOOPS

On one of the hoops, locate the splice or seam where the hoop has been put together. Make a mark 2" from this splice. From this mark measure the circumference of the hoop (8" hoop should measure about 25-1/2"). Divide the circumference in half, measure that distance from the first mark and mark again. See **Diagram 1**. This hoop will be your basket handle.

The area between the pencil marks (containing the splice) is the bottom of the handle. On the inside of the hoop, put your name or initial as shown in **Diagram 1**. On the second hoop, which will be the rim of the basket, measure and mark 2" from the splice and again at the halfway point on the hoop. This divides the hoop into two equal parts. Now, take the two hoops (handle and rim) and fit them together as in **Diagram 2**, sliding them until the pencil marks line up. Make sure that the handle hoop is on the outside of the rim hoop. Using waxed string, tie the hoops securely as in **Diagram 3**.

WEAVING THE GOD'S EYE

Select the 2 thinnest, most pliable weavers for making the God's Eye, making sure each is at least 8 feet long. Coil the strips separately and secure them with a bread tie or clothespin.

Soak both coils in warm water for 1 to 3 minutes. Check weavers and when they are pliable, remove from the water. Uncoil one to begin the God's Eye. Wrap the other in a towel until you are ready to begin the other side. *Note:* The flat reed has a right and a wrong side. The edges of the right side are slightly rounded or beveled. The wrong side has edges which are perfectly flat and is the rougher side. Begin the God's Eye by placing the wrong side against the hoops. When weaving the basket, you need not be concerned with the right and wrong sides.

Referring to **Diagram 4** and the instructions, start to weave. It may help to number the 4 hoop sections as shown. The God's Eye must be very flat. Pull weavers tight and press firmly as you make the revolutions, making sure the weaver is pressed completely flat against the hoop and the previous row. Use your thumbs to flatten weavers as you work.

Begin with the weaver on

Preliminary step to shape ribs

Diagram A

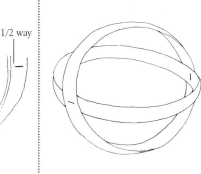

1/2 way   1/2 way

Splice

Name

Diagram 1

Diagram 2

The melon shape is probably one of the oldest of all ribbed baskets. It is also one of the easiest to make and thus an excellent beginner basket. The most obvious reason for its name is that it is shaped like a melon. Unlike the egg, which has a "fanny," or "buttocks," the melon has a perfectly round bottom. Natural materials such as honeysuckle, grapevine or wisteria make wonderful melon baskets. If you don't have access to any of our native naturals, consider a commercial "natural" like vine rattan. Instructions for using vine can be found at the end of the melon instructions.

APPROXIMATE SIZE

8" diameter

MATERIALS

Two 8" round hoops (frame)
1/2" flat reed (weavers)
3/8" flat oval reed, 3/8" oval oval, or #6 round reed (ribs)
1/4" flat reed (weavers)

top of the hoops at the dot. Move up and behind 1, diagonally to 2, behind 2, diagonally to 3, etc. From 4 move diagonally to 1 and repeat entire counterclockwise revolution 5 more times. You will notice that the starting point (end of reed) is covered as the weaver moves from 2 to 3.

The finished God's Eye will have 6 revolutions counting from the back and will look like **Diagram 5**. The God's Eye is flat to the touch. The weavers must not overlap each other, as any overlap will make the God's Eye bulky. From the back it will look like **Diagram 6**.

A good flat God's Eye is critical. The success of the basket depends on its construction. Don't be discouraged if your first try isn't perfect. Just take it out and try again. At the end of the sixth revolution, the weaver is behind 4. *Do not cut.* Secure with clothespin. Repeat God's Eye on the other side with other coiled weaver.

MAKING & INSERTING RIBS
Remove the ribs from the hoops and sharpen all the ends to a point with a knife or pencil sharpener.

Insert the primary ribs, one at a time, into the 2 God's

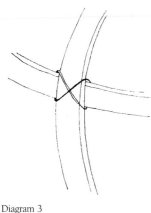

Diagram 3

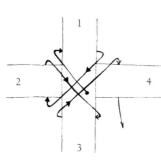

Diagram 4

Completed God's Eye with weaver uncut
Diagram 5

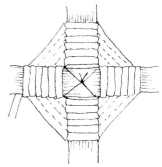

Inside view equal wraps on all 4 points
Diagram 6

Eyes. The ribs will slide in behind the eye in the pocket formed between the rim and the lowest part of the handle. See **Diagram 7**. *Note:* If you are using the oval or flat oval reed, taper the ends gradually with a knife for approximately 3".

WEAVING THE BASKET

Take the clothespin off only one of the weavers. If it is dry or stiff, rewet it. Begin weaving by going over rib 1, under rib 2, over rib 3, under the lower handle, over and under the remaining ribs until you reach the rim. This first row of weaving should be snug against the God's Eye. Bring the weaver up from the back, over the rim to the front, and begin the over and under pattern in the opposite direction. Refer to **Diagram 8**.

Note: The most important part of weaving is to push the weaver snugly against the previous row. Pulling the weavers hard is unnecessary and tends to misshape the ribs. The diagram shows weavers loosely woven to clearly illustrate the weaving pattern. Do not weave this loosely. Also, be careful to weave under 1 rib, over 1 rib, etc. If you weave over 2 ribs at any time, the alternating over-under pattern will be disrupted.

Weave 4 complete rows and clamp with clothespins. These first 4 rows anchor the primary ribs in place. However, they may still move and may slip out of place, so take care to check their position as you go along.

ADDING SECONDARY RIBS

You should have four 12" ribs left to insert. Add 1 rib between the first and second primary ribs, pushing the points (one end and then the other) into the same space with the first ribs. Be sure to conceal each point under a weaver. Add the other secondary rib between the second and third primary ribs, concealing the points as before. See **Diagram 9**.

With 4 rows of weaving complete on both sides and all 10 ribs in place, the basic skeleton of the melon basket should be obvious as in **Diagram 10**. At this point, make very sure that each of the 10 ribs follows the same curve and extends out the same distance as the hoops. It may be necessary to adjust rib lengths of ribs by pushing them further into the weaving or pulling them out slightly.

Note: The first row of weaving, after any new ribs are added, will alter the over-under pattern. Continue to weave in the over-under pattern *each* rib. The weaving will correct itself on the second row and a new pattern will be established.

SPLICING

When you have 2" or 3" of weaver left, it is time to join a new (soaked) weave to it. This joining should not take place at the rim, so backtrack if necessary. Referring to **Diagram 11**, overlap the new weaver on top of the old one. You will be weaving with 2 pieces of reed for 3 or 4 ribs. Hide the ends under a rib.

FINISHING THE BASKET

Continue weaving the basket, one side at a time. Do not weave all of one side, and then the other. Instead, weave 3 rows on one side then 3 rows on the other, to keep the basket balanced. Weave until both sides meet in the center. If there is a space that has not filled in, simply add a short weaver and fill in the space, making sure you end up with the over-under pattern on alternating rows. Push weavers out from the center to make room for last row if necessary.

MEASUREMENTS FOR OTHER SIZES OF MELON BASKETS

BASKET DIAMETER	PRIMARY RIBS	SECONDARY RIBS
6"	9"	7-1/2"
8"	12-1/2"	12"
10"	15-1/1"	14"
12"	19"	17-1/2"

MELON BASKET USING VINE RATTAN

Soak the entire coil of vine rattan. Almost impossible to separate when dry, one or two pieces can be pulled out easily when it is wet.

Make your own hoops from the vine rattan by forming a circle with one piece and wrapping other pieces around it until it is as thick as you want. Construct 2 hoops and fit one inside the other just as is described in the general instructions. Make the God's Eye with a long piece of rattan. Make "ribs" by twisting 2 or 3 pieces together as one. Splice a new piece on when an old one runs out as in **Diagram 12**.

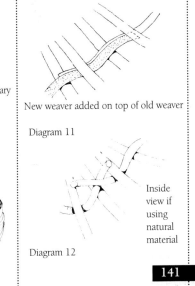

New weaver added on top of old weaver

Diagram 11

Inside view if using natural material

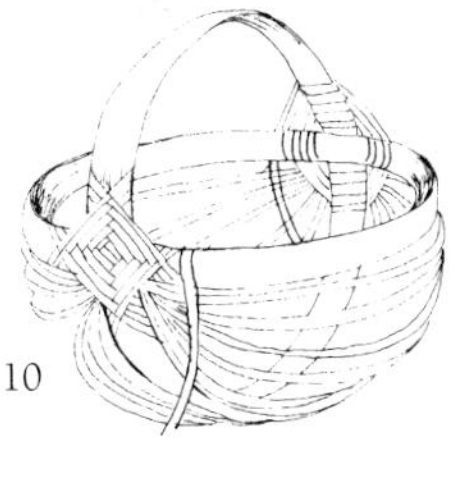

Diagram 12

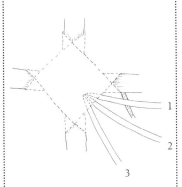

1

2

3

Diagram 7

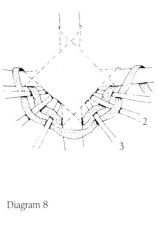

1

2

3

Diagram 8

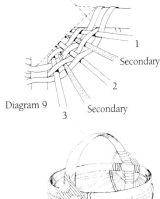

1

Secondary

2

Diagram 9

3

Secondary

Diagram 10

Bennett, Jim. *Handling White Oak,* 1985. Deer Track Crafts, 8215 Beeman Rd., Chelsea, MI 48118.

Boy Scouts of America. *Basketry,* 1968. Boy Scouts of America, Supply Division, Midwestern Distribution Center, 1930 North Mannheim Rd., Melrose Park, IL 60160.

Burr, Marion Sober. *Basket Patterns,* 1975. Available from the author, Box 294, Plymouth, MI 48170.

Cary, Mara. *Basic Baskets,* 1975. Boston: Houghton Mifflin.

Christopher, F.J. *Basketry,* 1952. New York: Dover Publishing Company.

Eaton, Allen H. *Handicrafts of the Southern Highlands,* 1973. New York: Dover Publishing Company.

Hart, Carol, and Dan Hart. *Natural Basketry,* 1976. New York: Watson-Guptill Publications.

Hoppe, Flo. *Wicker Basketry,* 1989. Interweave Press, 306 North Washington Ave., Loveland, CO 80537.

Horowitz, Elinor L. *Mountain People, Mountain Crafts,* 1974. New York: J. P. Lippincott Company.

Irwin, John Rice. *Baskets and Basketmakers in Southern Appalachia,* 1982. Schiffer Publishing Company, Box E, Exton, PA 19341.

Jacobs, Betty E.M. *Growing Herbs and Plants for Dyeing,* 1977. Select Books, Rt. 1, Box 129C, Mountain View, MO 65548.

Johnson, Kay. *Canework,* 1986. London: Dryad Press, Ltd.

La Plantz, Shereen. *Plaited Basketry: The Woven Form,* 1982. Press de La Plantz, 899 Bayside Cutoff, Bayside, CA 95524.

Larason, Lew. *The Basket Collector's Book,* 1978. Scorpio Publications, 2 East Butler St., Chalfont, PA 18914.

Lasansky, Jeanette. *Willow, Oak and Rye,* 1979. Keystone Books, Pennsylvania State University Press, 215 Wagner Building, University Park, PA 16802.

Pulleyn, Rob. *The Basketmaker's Art,* 1987. Lark Books, 50 College St., Asheville, NC 28801.

Schiffer, Nancy. *Baskets,* 1984. Schiffer Publishing Ltd., Box E, Exton, PA 19341.

Siler, Lyn. *The Basket Book,* 1988. Sterling Publishing Co., 387 Park Ave. South, New York, NY 10016.

Stephenson, Sue M. *Basketry of the Appalachian Mountains,* 1977. New York: Van Nostrand Reinhold Company.

Teleki, Gloria Roth. *The Baskets of Rural America,* 1975. New York: E.P. Dutton and Company.

Teleki, Gloria Roth. *Collecting Traditional Basketry,* 1979. New York: E. P. Dutton and Company.

Thompson, Frances. *Antique Baskets and Basketry,* 1985. Wallace- Homestead Book Company, 580 Waters Edge, Lombard, IL 60148.

_____. Wallace-Homestead Price *Guide to Baskets,* 1987. Wallace-Homestead Company, 580 Waters Edge, Lombard, IL 60148.

Tod, Osma Gallinger. *Earth Basketry,* 1972. New York: Crown Publishers.

Wright, Dorothy. *The Complete Book of Baskets and Basketry,* 1983. North Pomfret, Vermont: David and Charles, Inc.

Continued from page 8.

three-rod wale	Inserting three weavers, each behind three consecutive stakes, with all three weaving, one at a time, over two and under one.
true	To measure the woven base, making sure all sides are the correct length, adjusting if necessary and marking corners.
tucking in	When the basket is woven, the outside stakes are pointed, bent over and tucked into the weaving on the inside of the basket; also called down staking.
twill	A method of weaving in which the weaver passes over and under the stakes two at a time.
twining	A method of weaving in which two weavers are used alternately in a twisting pattern in front of one spoke and behind one spoke.
upsett or upstake	To bend the stakes up and over upon themselves (toward the base), creating a crease at the base of the stake.
wale	A method of weaving in which the left weaver is always moved over the weavers and spokes to the right, behind one and out to the front.
warp	The stationary, usually more rigid, element in weaving.
weaver	The fiber, often reed, used as the "weft" that moves over and under the stakes, spokes or ribs (warp).
weft	The more flexible weaving element that is interlaced around the warp.
wicker	From the Swedish vikker, meaning "willow" or "osier." Generally refers to any round, shoot-like material used for basketmaking.
wicker work	A basketry technique that employs round, vertical stakes or spokes, and round weavers which are woven perpendicular to the spokes.
willow	An osier which yields its long, slender branches for use in basket weaving.
wisteria	A climbing vine that is particularly flexible and used for basket weaving and for making basket handles.

Contributors

Kris Aymar, Glenwood MD
Sosse Baker, Chester, CT
Joyce Caldwell, Asheville, NC
Dianne Craver, Candler, NC
Janet Finger, Wilmar, MN
Patti Hawkins, Pace, FL
Patti Hill, Weaverville, NC
Jim Hoffman, Asheville, NC
Flo Hoppe, Rome, NY
Genie Jackson, Coral Springs, FL
Mark Katz, LaFarge, WI
Eileen Laporte, Romeo, MI
Joan Moore, Highland, MI
Theresa Ohno, Seattle, WA
Judith Olney, Rowley, MA
Debbie Richards, Lake Orion, MI
Cass Schorsch, Ludington, MI
Linda Scoggins, Fayetteville, NC
Dianne Stanton, Pembroke, MA
Jessie Stewart, Candler, NC
Larry Walther, Clyde, NC
Judy Wilson, Hiawasse, GA

Sources of Supply

Ewe 'n Me (Kris Aymar)
P.O. Box 13
Glenwood, MD 21738
Instructor, Baskets

Chester Gallery (Sosse Baker)
Chester, CT 06412
Instructor, Baskets

Dianne Craver
Rt.1, Box 561
Candler, NC 28715
Baskets

Janet Finger (Baskets Ltd.)
701 S.W. 18th St.
Wilmar, MN 56201
Instructor, Baskets

Patti Hawkins
5313 Rowe Trail
Pace, Fl 32571
Instructor, Patterns, Baskets

Flo Hoppe
221 Dale Rd.
Rome, NY 13440
Instructor, Baskets, Books

Genie Jackson
5055 NW 100th Terrace
Coral Springs, FL 33076
Instructor, Patterns, Baskets, Books

Crooked River Crafts (Mark Katz)
P.O.Box 917
La Farge, WI 54639
Instructor, Baskets, Dyes, Dyed Reed

Eileen LaPorte
8275 W. 31 Mile Rd.
Romeo, MI 48065
Instructor, Patterns, Baskets

JAM Creations (Joan Moore)
P.O. Box 764
Highland, MI 48357
Instructor, Baskets, Patterns, Books

Happenstance Basketry (Judith Olney)
34 Bradford St.
Rowley, MA 01969
Instructor, Baskets

Debbie Richards
535 Indianwood
Lake Orion, MI 48362
Instructor, Baskets, Patterns

Trillium Enterprises (Cass Schorsch)
6375 N. Maplewood Dr.
Ludington, MI 49431
Instructor, Birch (and Other) Bark
   Baskets

LS Basketry (Linda Scoggins)
6414 Barwick Dr.
Fayetteville, NC 28303
Instructor, Baskets, Patterns

The Weavery (Lyn Siler)
P.O. Box 1626
Weaverville, NC 28787
Instructor, Books, Specialty Handles
   and Tools, Spoke Weights, Space-
   Dyed Reed, General Supplies

Dianne Stanton
365 High St.
Pembroke, MA 02359
Instructor, Back Pack Straps,
   Diagonal Shears, Baskets

Baskets by Judy (Judy Wilson)
PO Box 1016
Hiawasse, GA 30546
Instructor, Multicolored Egg (and
   Other) Baskets

Dell Pickle
3210 E. 3rd St.
Brunswick, GA 31520
Pine Needles for Basketmaking

Jacob Young & Westbury
JYW House Bridge Road
Haywards Heath W.
Sussex, England RM16 IT2

Metric Conversion
INCHES TO CENTIMETERS

INCHES	CM	INCHES	CM
1/8	0.3	19	48.3
1/4	0.6	20	50.8
3/8	1.0	21	53.3
1/2	1.3	22	55.9
5/8	1.6	23	58.4
3/4	1.9	24	61.0
7/8	2.2	25	63.5
1	2.5	26	66.0
1-1/4	3.2	27	68.6
1-1/2	3.8	28	71.1
1-3/4	4.4	29	73.7
2	5.1	30	76.2
2-1/2	6.4	31	78.7
3	7.6	32	81.3
3-1/2	8.9	33	83.8
4	10.2	34	86.4
4-1/2	11.4	35	88.9
5	12.7	36	91.4
6	15.2	37	94.0
7	17.8	38	96.5
8	20.3	39	99.1
9	22.9	40	101.6
10	25.4	41	104.1
11	27.9	42	106.7
12	30.5	43	109.2
13	33.0	44	111.8
14	35.6	45	114.3
15	38.1	46	116.8
16	40.6	47	119.4
17	43.2	48	121.9
18	45.7	49	124.5
		50	127.0

I N D E X

Location Photography

We would like to thank the generous people who allowed us to bring lights, cameras, props, photographers, art directors, designers, editors, and confusion into their homes or their businesses or both.

John Cram
The Blue Spiral Gallery
Asheville, North Carolina
Page 89.

Edd and Peggy Elkins
Elkins Antiques
Weaverville, North Carolina
Pages 31 and 53.

John and Patti Hill (and Cleo)
Weaverville, North Carolina
Pages 125 and 129.

Alison Hinman
The Smith-McDowell Museum
Asheville, North Carolina
Pages 101 and 112.

Rick and Jane Morgan
Marshall, North Carolina
Pages 23 and 39.

Frank and Flo Wallin
Weaverville, North Carolina
Page 57.

Tom and Jan Weil
Asheville, North Carolina
Page 73.

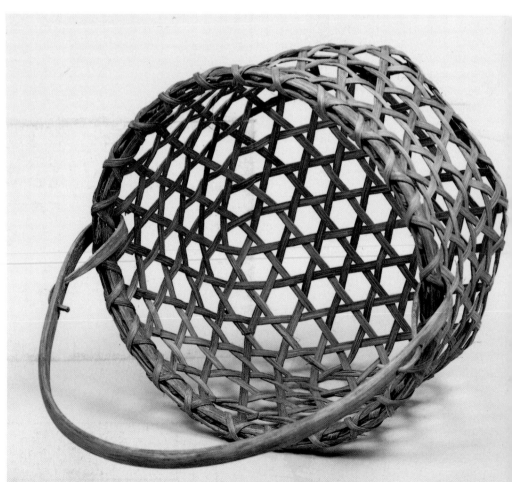